HOPE AMID
THE RUINS

HOPE AMID THE RUINS

The Ethics of Israel's Prophets

Carol J. Dempsey

St. Louis, Missouri

Biblical quotations, unless otherwise noted, are from the *New Revised Standard Version Bible*, copyright 1989, Division of Christian Education of the National Council of Churches of Christ in the United States of America. Used by permission. All rights reserved.

Cover photo: © PhotoDisc
Cover design: Elaine Young
Interior design: Wynn Younker
Art direction: Michael Domínguez

This book is printed on acid-free, recycled paper.

Visit Chalice Press on the World Wide Web at
www.chalicepress.com

10 9 8 7 6 5 4 3 2 1   00 01 02 03

Library of Congress Cataloging–in–Publication Data

Dempsey, Carol J.
   Hope amid the ruins : the ethics of Israel's prophets / Carol J. Dempsey.
      p.   cm.
   Includes bibliographical references and index.
   ISBN 0-8272-1439-1
   1. Bible O.T. Prophets—Criticism, interpretation, etc. 2. Ethics in the Bible.
I. Title.
   BS1505 .2 D455   2000
    241.5—dc21   00-010032

To my sister Kathy and my brother-in-law Kevin,
and to my brother George and my sister-in-law Jenni,
whose love and commitment have blessed me
with my niece, Shannon, and my nephews Scott, Kenny, Gary,
Tyler, Travis, Trent, and Traig, in whose eyes and hearts I see the beauty of God
and hope for the new day dawning.

Contents

Abbreviations

AB	Anchor Bible
ANET	*Ancient Near Eastern Texts,* ed. J. B. Pritchard, 3d ed.
ATR	*Anglican Theological Review*
BDB	F. Brown, S. R. Driver, and C. A. Briggs, *Hebrew and English Lexicon of the Old Testament*
BTB	*Biblical Theology Bulletin*
CBC	Cambridge Bible Commentary
CBQ	*Catholic Biblical Quarterly*
CCA	Continental Commentaries from Augsburg
FCB	Feminist Companion to the Bible
FOTL	Forms of the Old Testament Literature
ICC	International Critical Commentary
IDB	*Interpreter's Dictionary of the Bible,* ed. G. A. Buttrick
ITC	International Theological Commentary
JLR	*Journal of Law and Religion*
JSOTSup	*Journal for the Study of the Old Testament* Supplement Series
MT	Masoretic Text
NAC	New American Commentary
NCBC	New Century Bible Commentary
NICOT	New International Commentary on the Old Testament
NJBC	*The New Jerome Biblical Commentary,* ed. R. E. Brown, et al.
NSBT	New Studies in Biblical Theology
OBT	Overtures to Biblical Theology
OTG	Old Testament Guides
OTM	Old Testament Message
SBLDS	Society of Biblical Literature Dissertation Series
VT	*Vetus Testamentum*
WestBC	Westminster Bible Companion
WordBC	Word Biblical Commentary

Preface

No creation ever comes to life without the help and support of others who give generously of their time and labor. Thus, I would now like to acknowledge those who have helped with the creative process of this work. To my friends and colleagues Chris Franke and Ehud Ben Zvi, whose great love of and work on the prophets continue to inspire and inform my own work, I extend a hearty thank-you.

To my colleagues in the Feminist Hermeneutics Task Force section of the Catholic Biblical Association, in particular Sandra Schneiders, Kathleen O'Connor, Mary Rose D'Angelo, Judith Schubert, Barbara Bowe, Mary Margaret Pazdan, Alice Laffey, Linda Maloney, Amy-Jill Levine, Barbara Reid, Sheila McGinn, Barbara Green, and others with whom I have worked for the past six years, whose biblical, theological, and hermeneutical probings and work have given expression to a concern for all creation. They have kept the prophetic vision ever before me, and I owe them my deep gratitude.

I am also grateful to my colleagues at the University of Portland, in particular those members of my department, especially Russell Butkus and Matthew Baasten, whose conversations about the prophets, ethics, and new paradigms have refined my own thinking, and to Marlene Moore, Dean of the College of Arts and Sciences, for her continual support and enthusiastic encouragement of research projects and creative endeavors. To Vickie Hamilton, Caroline Mann, Carol Leatherman, Carolyn Piatz, and the entire library staff, for processing my research requests and helping me to access the materials I needed, and to the University Committee on Teaching and Scholarship, who granted me a Faculty Research Award that made available time and funds to complete this project, I express my thanks.

To my editor, Jon L. Berquist, for his gracious support, his helpful advice and insights, his careful reading of the manuscript, his patience, and his firm commitment to this project from the time of its planning through its publication, and to all at Chalice Press for their efforts, I am grateful.

Finally, I want to express my deepest appreciation to Seth Patla, a graduated theology major of the University of Portland who typed this entire manuscript and added many wonderful and insightful editorial suggestions. My gratitude for the care and interest that he gave to this work is without adequate expression. His faithfulness to the task at hand, his biblical and theological astuteness, and his good humor throughout the project made the writing and discussion of ideas most enjoyable.

I would be remiss if I did not add a special note of thanks to my little Zebra Finches, Noel and Joel, who sang me through the work and who continually remind me about my covenant with the birds of the air and all God's creation.

To all, I offer my gratitude and my blessing.

April 23, 2000
Easter

Introduction

To an ancient Israelite people and land waiting for redemption and restoration, the words of the prophet Isaiah are a welcome message:

For I am about to create new heavens
and a new earth;
the former things shall not be remembered
or come to mind. (Isa. 65:17)

Creator God is going to do something new. Thus, the prophet's words offer a vision, a sense of hope. This vision, this sense of hope transcends time, space, and generations.

The divine words of Isaiah offer hope and challenge to a people and world today that have left behind a century and a millennium characterized by tremendous technological advancements yet plagued by unforgettable atomic devastation, a Holocaust, wars, and multilayered violence, along with political, economic, and social structures in sore need of transformation and environmental questions and problems left largely unanswered and unresolved.

The human community and all creation have stepped into a new century and a new millennium bright with promise and ripe with opportunity. Now, more than ever, the human community has the challenge to till and care for all creation so that all creation may enjoy the continued gift of life, life that is characterized by justice, righteousness, and loving-kindness attained through ethical practice. Only then will the envisioned new heavens and new earth emerge from the ruins of the past and hope become something more than a grace received.

This volume aims to retrieve, critique, and then reread the ethics of Israel's prophets. Proceeding from a thematic and reader-centered approach

1

and informed by contemporary ideological, social, and ecological concerns, the study is divided into seven chapters. Chapter 1 highlights recent biblical scholarship on prophetic ethics. Chapter 2 situates and explores the ethics of Israel's prophets in relation to creation and covenant and asserts that the notion of "relationship" is integral to the prophets' ethical vision. Chapter 3 considers Torah as a way of life that grounds the prophets' ethical vision in justice, righteousness, and loving-kindness. Chapters 4 and 5 examine in detail selected texts from the prophets in order to unveil the prophets' ethical concerns and to critique the ethics of their message in light of contemporary questions and concerns. Chapter 6 focuses on the theme of worship and highlights the shift from worship as ritual practices to worship as ethical practices, a vision embedded in various prophetic texts. Finally, chapter 7 looks at the relationship between the redemption of humankind and the restoration of creation and the prophetic challenges that face the human community. The work closes with a brief epilogue that offers a word of hope.

This work not only looks at the ethics of Israel's prophets but also calls the prophets' ethical message into question. Thus, the work is both critical and hermeneutical. The volume is ordered according to themes. Prophetic books and texts are not studied in the order in which they appear in the canon; no single prophetic book is studied in its entirety; and not all prophetic books are included in the study. Passages are selected and arranged according to various themes developed in each of the seven chapters. Certain passages from the Pentateuch are included for the purpose of establishing the background and a link to the prophets' ethical vision. Furthermore, the study is concerned with the final canonical form of each prophetic text, not with the texts' various stages of development, transmission, and redaction.

Central to the discussion of the prophets' ethics is the multifaceted way that God is portrayed by the prophetic texts. Because these texts have gone through a long oral and written transmission process, what readers now see and hear is not the actual voice of God but rather the voices of prophets, authors, redactors, and final editors, who try to communicate their experience of history and their experience of God. What should be remembered is that what has been recorded is historically, socially, culturally, and theologically conditioned, a characteristic of the entire biblical text.

One final word: This volume aims to reread the ethics of Israel's prophets so that a new vision for all creation can blossom. In the fertile ground of the past lie the dormant seeds of hope for the present, waiting to burst into life with the coming of the spring rains as all creation reaches out to embrace the birth of this new century, this new millennium—both of which remain pregnant with possibilities. Would that the restored and renewed ethical vision of Israel's prophets become a true source of power for the journey from light into Light.

Chapter 1

Old Testament Ethics and the Prophets' Ethical Vision

A Review and Reassessment

Old Testament ethics continue to engage biblical scholars in discourse and debate, and the connection between prophecy and ethics is of equal interest. In recent years scholars have produced major works in both areas, but more work remains to be done, particularly in the area of prophecy and ethics. The exploration of new paradigms provides new critical and hermeneutical questions that can help readers evaluate the ethics of the ethical message of the prophets. This study presents new paradigms while raising new questions to advance the conversation on prophecy and ethics in directions shaped by the recent contributions of several scholars of Old Testament ethics and prophetic ethics. Since the publication of Walter C. Kaiser, Jr.'s, study *Toward Old Testament Ethics* (1983),[1] five other major works pertaining to Old Testament ethics have appeared.

Bruce C. Birch

The first of these works, *Let Justice Roll Down: The Old Testament, Ethics, and Christian Life* (1991)[2] by Bruce C. Birch, is divided into two parts and nine chapters. This extensive study explores a variety of topics pertinent to ethics and the Old Testament. In his introduction, Birch establishes his basic premise and argument, namely, that the Old Testament plays a significant role in the shaping of the moral and ethical character of

---

[1] Walter C. Kaiser, Jr., *Toward Old Testament Ethics* (Grand Rapids, Mich.: Zondervan, 1983).

[2] Bruce C. Birch, *Let Justice Roll Down: The Old Testament, Ethics, and Christian Life* (Louisville, Ky.: Westminster/John Knox Press, 1991).

the Christian community. After a series of disclaimers of what his study is not,[3] Birch admits that his primary interest is to clarify and make available "the Old Testament witness that should inform the Church on the entire range of moral issues that might be faced in the course of Christian life."[4] Despite these disclaimers, Birch's work does deal in detail with a variety of topics that are essential to establishing an understanding of ancient Israelite life and its ethical demands.

In the first part of his study, "Method and Approach," Birch considers how the Old Testament has made a contribution to Christian ethics. Birch comments on community; moral agency; biblical authority; morality in ancient Israel; the will, activity, and character of God; the role and importance of canon; and Old Testament narrative and moral address.[5]

In the second part of his study, "The Old Testament Story as Moral Resource," Birch explores several topics that contribute to a firm understanding of Old Testament ethics. He begins this section with a discussion on the Creator and creation and focuses on God as the one who creates and blesses. He argues that the Old Testament presents a portrait of God not only as sovereign Creator but also as one who is intimately involved with creation. Birch contends that benevolence, relationality, and wholeness characterize creation. "As good, the creation is declared to be in harmony with the divine intention."[6] He makes the striking point that "in creation all things are related. No element of God's creation, including the human, is self-sufficient. In creation we are related to God, to others, and to the rest of nature."[7] Furthermore, Birch asserts that "closely related to benevolence and relationality is God's intention that creation be whole and harmonious."[8] Birch grounds the prophets' ethical vision in creation, covenant, and the understanding of relationality, as I do in chapter 2.

Birch next discusses the ideas of dominion and stewardship as divine attributes to be charged to the Judeo-Christian tradition, particularly in this current time of ecological crisis. He closes his discussion on creation with a comment on grace and redemption and claims that "we are reminded that God as Creator still sustains the creation, but we are given

---

[3]Ibid. Birch states that his work "is *not* a book on Old Testament ethics" (p. 19), "is *not* an attempt to write the ethics of the Old Testament" (p. 19), is "*not* an introductory text or an attempt at the comprehensive survey of the subject" (p. 19), and is "*not* intended to address topical issues in the life of the Church" (p. 20).

[4]Ibid., 20.

[5]For further discussion see ibid., 29–68.

[6]Ibid., 81.

[7]Ibid., 82.

[8]Ibid., 83.

our first glimpses of a God who also chooses to be active within creation for the sake of redeeming it."[9] I explore in detail Birch's idea of creation's redemption in chapter 6, which links cosmic redemption to the redemption of humanity and the restoration of the natural world, because in the end all creation will be redeemed.

In subsequent chapters, Birch looks at the themes of promise and deliverance in Genesis and Exodus and then describes the birth of the Israelite community. In his discussion on "People of the Covenant," Birch stresses that God, who is holy, merciful, faithful, righteous, and just, is the initiator of covenants in the Old Testament. He points out that covenant and Torah helped shape Israel's life in the land and as a community. Having established those key themes, specifically creation, covenant, and Torah, which played a significant role in the life of the Israelite community, Birch next looks at these concepts among others in conjunction with the monarchy, the prophets, and the wisdom tradition. He closes his work with a brief epilogue in which he concludes that there is a "continuity of God's grace," a "continuity of God's people," and a "continuity of God's work."[10]

Concerning the ethics of Israel's prophets, Birch accents the idea of relationality in the development of Old Testament ethics. Affirming the importance of covenant and law as essential to an ethical way of life, Birch focuses on God as creator and God's relationship to and with creation. Thus, he integrates covenant and law so that readers can appreciate Old Testament ethics as something far greater and much more important than adherence to a moral or legal code that aims solely for the preservation, sustenance, and redemption of human life. Birch challenges those who view Old Testament ethics from an anthropocentric perspective, and his work lays a foundation for this present work to re-vision prophetic ethics with its attempt to articulate a new ethical way of life for the benefit of all creation.

Waldemar Janzen

A work on Old Testament ethics that appeared after Birch's study is *Old Testament Ethics: A Paradigmatic Approach* by Waldemar Janzen (1994).[11] Sharing Birch's concern that such scholarship inform the church community, Janzen's book aims to speak "to the church,"[12] and "it addresses

---

[9]Ibid., 97.

[10]For a more detailed discussion of these ideas, see ibid., 356–57.

[11]Waldemar Janzen, *Old Testament Ethics: A Paradigmatic Approach* (Louisville, Ky.: Westminster/John Knox Press, 1994).

[12]Ibid., 1.

Christians who have the Old Testament before them in its entirety and accept it as part of their canon."[13] Sharing similar goals and views with Birch's work, yet divergent and distinct from it, especially in its approach, Janzen's study begins with the genre of story instead of a focus on law. He argues that "story in the literary genre,…next to actual cultic practice, was most important in the transmission of theological-ethical instruction in ancient Israel itself."[14]

In his initial chapter, Janzen analyzes five stories, each of which claims to model right ethical behavior. In the course of his analysis, he suggests that stories shape paradigms. He then clarifies the meaning and function of a paradigm and identifies the familial paradigm as primary, with four others that are associated with it but subordinate to it. These include the priestly, wisdom, royal, and prophetic paradigms. In chapter 2 Janzen looks at the familial paradigm in detail and draws particular attention to Genesis 13 and the Abraham story, the book of Ruth, and Judges 19. In Janzen's view, life, land, and hospitality are three elements essential to the familial paradigm. Based on his analysis of these three works, he concludes that rooted in the biblical story is an ethic that can be uncovered.

Continuing with his triad of life, land, and hospitality and his claim that intrinsic to the biblical study is an ethic, Janzen stresses in chapter 3 that "the ethical reality continues to reside in [the stories], rather than in a general formulation abstracted from or illustrated by them."[15] The remainder of the chapter explores the topic of law as principle and as story. Janzen argues for the primacy of story over law when dealing with Old Testament ethics and repeats his argument against a reductionist use of principles that would limit one's understanding of Old Testament ethics to what can be extrapolated from a text. Janzen rightfully insists that laws and ethics are embedded in the biblical story.

In chapter 4, Janzen addresses the topic of the Decalogue, and after presenting its historical context, its social value, how scholars have tended to view it, and its context, Janzen makes the claim that "the Decalogue should not be equated with a comprehensive coverage of the whole Old Testament (or Christian, or universal human) ethics."[16] He connects the Decalogue to the familial paradigm and reexamines its content from this perspective, noting its powerful familial thrust. Janzen affirms the Decalogue's centrality of peace and function within the covenant story but warns against isolating these laws from their narrative context so as to

---

[13]Ibid.
[14]Ibid., 2.
[15]Ibid., 56.
[16]Ibid., 95.

make them a comprehensive legal scheme or a universal ethical teaching that becomes an end in itself.

In the next two chapters, Janzen discusses the priestly and wisdom paradigms (chapter 5) and the royal and prophetic paradigms (chapter 6) in relation to selected Old Testament biblical narratives. In his final chapter (chapter 7), he uses the canonical approach to link the Old and New Testaments in a modified way to determine "what the nature of the impact of the New Testament on [his] Old Testament findings might be."[17] Janzen specifically looks at his proposed Old Testament paradigms in the light of the paradigm of Jesus as priest, sage, king, and prophet. He then comments on the paradigmatic roles of Jesus and highlights their centrality to the proclamation of the kingdom of God. Finally, he connects ideas about the kingdom of God to the familial paradigm and takes another look at the triad concepts of life, land, and hospitality in this new context. What Janzen discovers is that there is not only a significant relationship between the two testaments but also an ethical thrust contained within both canons' stories that could pave the way for the emergence of a "biblical ethics," while at the same time firmly grounding both the New Testament canon and the Christian community in a comprehensive understanding of ethics that could add to the shaping of Christian life, both individually and communally.

Janzen's claim that an ethic is rooted in the biblical story and his caution against reducing Old Testament ethics to what one can extrapolate from a text by way of an ethical message make significant contributions to this present study on prophetic ethics. Concerned not only with the historical context of the prophets' message but also with the literary aspects, this study seeks to search for and uncover an ethic within the prosaic and poetic material of the prophets for the purpose of not only articulating their ethical vision for their day but also for evaluating how ethical their ethics and ethical message were so that from their message, a vision can be retrieved that can offer direction and hope for all creation today.

Moshe Weinfeld

In 1995 Moshe Weinfeld published *Social Justice in Ancient Israel and in the Ancient Near East*.[18] Different from both Birch's work and Janzen's, Weinfeld's study focuses on one particular dimension of ethics—social justice—and includes not only the Old Testament but also the ancient Near East. Weinfeld's primary aim is to clarify the terms *justice* and

[17]Ibid., p. 188.
[18]Moshe Weinfeld, *Social Justice in Ancient Israel and in the Ancient Near East* (Minneapolis: Fortress Press, 1995).

righteousness and "especially the meaning of the expression… 'doing Justice and Righteousness.'"[19]

After a brief introduction, Weinfeld defines justice and righteousness in chapter 1 and then describes how these two virtues are the task of the king (chapter 2), the eschatological king (chapter 3), and the individual (chapter 10). He gives considerable attention to the topic of freedom in chapters 4, 5, 6, and 7, and to the sabbatical year and jubilee in chapter 8. In chapter 9 Weinfeld focuses on justice and righteousness as hallmarks of God's judgment, law, and reign. Through a careful reading of the text, Weinfeld is able to argue cogently that God's justice and righteousness were manifest at the time of creation and at the time of the exodus from Egypt, and will continue to be experienced in the messianic future when God will reign throughout the entire earth.[20] In the final chapter of his work (chapter 11), Weinfeld develops the theme of the Israelites as servants of YHWH and their land as belonging to YHWH. He views both these ideas in relation to the prevailing legal situation of the day and according to the notion of redemption as it unfolds in the Old Testament biblical tradition.

Weinfeld's understanding of justice and righteousness as concepts and as ethical practices, along with his focus on social justice, helps establish a foundation for further discussion of these three concepts as they pertain to Israel's prophets and this study, which seeks to present and evaluate the prophets' ethical message. Furthermore, I will expand on Weinfeld's notion of social justice, servanthood, and redemption to argue that within the writings of the prophets is the suggestion of a cosmic ethical vision.

Bruce V. Malchow

Building on Weinfeld's work and views on social justice, Bruce V. Malchow published *Social Justice in the Hebrew Bible* in 1996.[21] By opening his book with the comment that "social injustice is a major problem facing the world today,"[22] Malchow sets his remarks in a contemporary context and aims at addressing a wide audience. Like Weinfeld, he makes clear that social justice did not originate with Israel; it was a concern in the ancient Near Eastern world as a whole. Malchow points out that in dealing with its problems of injustice, Israel combined its own approach with traditions of the ancient Near East.

---

[19]Ibid., 5.

[20]For further discussion of justice and righteousness in relation to the ancient Near Eastern world, the life of the Israelite people, and the reign of God, see ibid., 179–214.

[21]Bruce V. Malchow, *Social Justice in the Hebrew Bible* (Collegeville, Minn.: Liturgical Press, 1996).

[22]Ibid., xi.

In chapter 1 Malchow links some of Israel's ethical policies to those that existed in the ancient Near East.[23] He then moves to the exodus event to capitalize on Israel's understanding of social injustice, an understanding gleaned from its experience of oppression in Egypt and its delivery from it by God, who then entered into covenant with the people and entrusted the Law to them. For Israel, then, its concern for social justice grew out of its cultural and life experiences.

Following the discussion on social justice as one of Israel's major concerns is a discussion in chapter 2 on the social setting of Israel's concern. Here Malchow focuses on Israel's class structure; those who were considered deprived in the society, such as widows, fatherless children, and sojourners; Israel's legal process; and the responsibility the monarch had to uphold justice. Malchow also briefly comments on the meaning of justice and righteousness in the Hebrew Bible.

In chapter 3 Malchow presents an overview of the biblical law codes and draws particular attention to those that promote social justice. In the remaining four chapters he looks at social justice as a theme in the prophetic books, the psalms, late narrative works, and wisdom literature. In the conclusion Malchow synthesizes his study and returns to his initial sentiment: "Social injustice is an immense and world-wide problem."[24] He is confident, though, that like the ancient Israelites, Christians today will tackle this problem with other people so that they "will achieve new thought and action together with them."[25]

Malchow's theme of social justice becomes a topic of discussion in this study on the ethics of Israel's prophets, and his research on various biblical law codes helps shape the study's concept of Torah as it applies to Israel's prophetic literature. His chapter on the prophetic books uncovers salient examples of social injustices that existed in Israel, particularly in the eighth century B.C.E. These and other examples are included and developed further in this work on prophetic ethics, which looks at the question of justice in its broadest context.

John Barton

Moving from the more defined category of social justice in the Hebrew Bible, John Barton, like Birch and Janzen, seeks to probe the more expansive topic of ethics in the Old Testament. His work *Ethics and the Old Testament*

---

[23]For example, the Near Eastern cultures surrounding Israel were concerned about protection for the poor, widows, and fatherless children, as well as care for the weak members of a group of people. Such concerns were found in Mesopotamia and Egypt, respectively, and were also Israel's concerns. See ibid., 1–5.

[24]Ibid., 78; compare xi.

[25]Ibid.

(1998)[26] is an edited compilation of the John Albert Hall lectures he gave in Victoria, Canada, in 1997. From the outset of his study, Barton acknowledges the difficulties involved with trying to articulate the relevance of Old Testament ethics for life today. He fully understands the problems that exist when one tries to make sense out of ancient moral injunctions that, in many cases, neither fit with nor are applicable to a contemporary audience with a modern worldview and life and cultural experiences years removed from the life experiences of the early Israelite community.

Although cognizant of such differences, Barton adopts the views and model of Martha C. Nussbaum[27] and argues that the ancient Israelite people and their writings can be conversation partners with us and can impart ethical wisdom because, even though the Israelites were very different from us in time and culture, they were dealing with many of the same life situations that we are dealing with today.

Like Janzen, Barton stresses that a "concentration on law does not do justice to what the Old Testament has to say about ethical questions,"[28] and he focuses on the role of story and its relation to ethics. For Barton, "stories can feed our moral life by providing us with visions of how real human beings can live through various crises and trials and remain human, that is, recognizably continuous with ourselves as part of the human race."[29] Barton states further that "general moral principles are found to operate in such stories, and they can be extracted and discussed."[30]

Unlike Birch, Janzen, Weinfeld, and Malchow, Barton looks at three contemporary ethical issues in relation to Old Testament ethics: ecology, sexual morality, and property. In each instance, Barton evaluates what the Old Testament states about these three issues and concludes that the text presents some ideas that are positive and helpful for today's world and other ideas that are just not applicable to the present-day world and its culture. Barton is the first writer mentioned thus far who engages in a critical hermeneutic of the biblical text.

Two final points that Barton considers in his study are natural law and morality. With respect to natural law, Barton concludes that "there is a great deal of natural law in the Old Testament, and that something like

---

[26]John Barton, *Ethics and the Old Testament* (London: SCM Press, 1998).

[27]Martha C. Nussbaum is known for her novel approach to moral philosophy. Nussbaum focuses on the particular and the individual wherein lies, according to her reasoning and investigation, the ingredients necessary for moral discernment. Her works include *The Fragility of Goodness: Luck and Ethics in Greek Tragedy and Philosophy* (Cambridge: Cambridge University Press, 1986); and *Love's Knowledge: Essays on Philosophy and Literature* (Oxford: Oxford University Press, 1990).

[28]Barton, *Ethics and the Old Testament*, 20.

[29]Ibid., 31.

[30]Ibid., 36.

this is the basis for ethics not only in rather sophisticated thinkers such as the prophets, but also at an underlying level in texts which go back to a pre-intellectual stage."[31] On the topic of morality, Barton finds that the Old Testament presents "quasi-philosophical lines of thought" rather than a specific "assertion" or "diktat."[32] Hence, the Old Testament tends to evoke a sense of morality rather than lay out specific guidelines or ways to be moral.

Barton's study reaffirms the importance and vitality of Old Testament ethics, and like Janzen's work, draws attention to the particular role that the biblical text as story plays in uncovering an ethical vision that lies within the stories themselves. Thus, Barton's work contributes to this present study on prophetic ethics with its focus on the biblical texts of the prophets and the ethics that lie within them. More importantly, Barton's critique of the biblical text in the light of contemporary ethical issues sets the stage for new ground to be broken by way of prophetic ethics and hermeneutics, which this present study hopes to do.

Eryl W. Davies

In addition to these five books on Old Testament ethics, four other works on Old Testament prophets and ethics have made significant contributions to the conversation about biblical and prophetic ethics. Eryl W. Davies' study on *Prophecy and Ethics: Isaiah and the Ethical Tradition of Israel* (1981)[33] is one of the few attempts made in recent years to study Old Testament ethics as they relate to the eighth-century prophets. Davies uses a form-critical methodology to analyze selected passages from Isaiah. His primary focus is on "the presence and use of traditional themes and motifs in the preaching of the prophets."[34]

The first chapter of Davies' work traces scholarly contributions on prophetic ethics, beginning with J. Wellhausen and B. Duhm.[35] His next three chapters examine specific ethical issues in Isaiah: Israel's rebellion against Yahweh (Isa. 1:2–3); the acquisition of land (Isa. 5:8–10); and the administration of justice (Isa. 1:21–26). Davies shows a relationship between prophecy and ethics and, by analyzing representative sections of Isaiah, demonstrates how ethical issues play an important role in that eighth-century prophet's overall message. Davies refutes that the Sinaitic covenant

---

[31]Ibid., 71.

[32]Ibid., 97.

[33]Eryl W. Davies, *Prophecy and Ethics: Isaiah and the Ethical Tradition of Israel*, JSOTSup 16 (Sheffield: JSOT Press, 1981).

[34]Ibid., 9.

[35]Ibid., 12–39.

influenced the thought and vocabulary of Isaiah, that the prophets appealed directly to the Law, that the wisdom tradition had a direct influence on prophecy, and that Isaiah was dependent on the oracles of Amos for some of his oracles.

Davies' study advances the discussion on prophecy and ethics, a subdivision of Old Testament ethics. The three selected Isaiah passages that he analyzes are either included or referred to in chapter 4, where selected prophetic texts are examined in an effort to bring examples of injustice and ethical issues to the fore. Of interest is that in Davies' analyses of the passages, he makes no reference to how ethical the prophet's message is, nor does he draw out any points for further consideration, as I will in subsequent chapters.

John Andrew Dearman

A second work concerned with a particular ethical point involving the eighth-century prophets is John Andrew Dearman's *Property Rights in the Eighth-Century Prophets: The Conflict and Its Background* (1988).[36] In his study, Dearman investigates the topic of property rights in Amos, Hosea, Isaiah, and Micah. He begins with a survey of scholars, such as Franz Walter, Albrecht Alt, Klaus Koch, and Oswald Loretz, whose work is closely related to the subject of property rights in the prophetic literature. He next locates all the references to property rights in the prophetic literature that can be dated to the eighth century B.C.E. and then does a thorough analysis of each reference. Two key questions that drive Dearman's study are: What are the fundamental or primary rights referred to or assumed when property is mentioned? and Who is responsible, if anyone, for their violation or administration?[37]

Dearman discovers that for the eighth-century prophets, property rights were often associated with some sort of socioeconomic conflict, and that the conflict over property rights was the result of several factors, including "privileges accorded to royal officials and the developing power of the administrative/judicial system which could be used by these officials and other persons for their benefit."[38]

Dearman makes several contributions to studies on prophecy and ethics. In particular, he illuminates the relationship between prophecy and ethics; demonstrates how one ethical issue—property rights—was a major concern for Amos, Hosea, Isaiah, and Micah; and furthers the

---

[36]John Andrew Dearman, *Property Rights in the Eighth-Century Prophets: The Conflict and Its Background*, SBLDS 106 (Atlanta: Scholars Press, 1988).

[37]Ibid., 16.

[38]Ibid., 149.

interpretation of the eighth-century prophetic texts. Like Davies, Dearman brings to the fore an important ethical issue that I will allude to later. However, more work needs to be done with respect to an exegetical as well as hermeneutical analysis of texts to surface not only ethical topics contained within them but also ethical issues that they raise and that call for further consideration.

G. Witaszek

Another brief yet substantial work on prophecy and ethics is that of G. Witaszek in 1992 titled *Provocy Amos i Micheasz wobec niesprawiedli wosci spolecznej*.[39] Witaszek focuses on social justice in Amos and Micah. He looks at specific texts within each book and then compares Micah's and Amos' critiques of the political, social, economic, and religious context. One of his conclusions is that many of the problems of injustice in Micah's and Amos' day stemmed from a shift in Israel's and Judah's lifestyle. Witaszek's discussion of social justice in relation to Micah and Amos contributes to the discussion of social justice in chapter 4. However, as did those scholars before him dealing with prophetic ethics, Witaszek leaves the door wide open for further consideration of the Micah and Amos texts, particularly because both books contain some graphic images that warrant comment from a contemporary ethical perspective.

Hemchand Gossai

Finally, *Justice, Righteousness and the Social Critique of the Eighth-Century Prophets* by Hemchand Gossai (1993)[40] is an extensive study on the concepts of justice and righteousness in the context of the ancient Near East, the Old Testament, and the eighth-century prophets. Gossai is meticulous not only in research and presentation of these terms but also in his ability to shed light on the relationship that justice has to righteousness in Old Testament contexts both exclusive and inclusive of the eighth-century prophets.

In addition to his comprehensive study of justice and righteousness as they appear in ancient Near East and Old Testament texts and the writings of the prophets, Gossai's last two chapters make a notable contribution to this present study on prophetic ethics. In his final two chapters, Gossai identifies the role and function of the eighth-century prophets[41] and then

---

[39]G. Witaszek, *Provocy Amos i Micheasz wobec niesprawiedli wosci spolecznej* (Tuchow: Mala Poligrafia oo. Redemtorystow, 1992).

[40]Hemchand Gossai, *Justice, Righteousness and the Social Critique of the Eighth-Century Prophets*, American University Studies Series no. 7, Theology and Religion, vol. 141 (New York: Peter Lang, 1993).

[41]For a detailed discussion, see ibid., 221–41.

looks at justice and righteousness in conjunction with a social critique of the eighth-century prophets and the intertwining of socioeconomic and cultic expectations.[42] Before presenting a series of elements of social critique, he argues that

> the critique by the Eighth Century prophets covers several aspects of the social, economic, and cultic life of Israel, all of which are intricately tied together. One of the critical elements which must be noted right at the outset is the fact that the basis of the brokenness within society can be traced to a brokenness in the people's relationship with Yahweh.[43]

This point is central to this present study on prophetic ethics, which seeks to suggest that at the heart of an ethical attitude and an ethical way of life is not one's understanding or keeping of covenant or the law but how well one understands relationship, beginning with an understanding of God's relationship to and with creation.

Conclusion

In summary, each of the nine scholars mentioned has involved and advanced in his own way the conversation about Old Testament ethics in general and prophetic ethics in particular. Collectively their research and insights have established important groundwork. Utilizing and building on the knowledge of these scholars, this study shifts in a new direction, beginning with a focus on "relationships" that leads not only to exposing the ethical issues of the prophets' day but also those embedded within the prophets' ethical message itself. This is a point that current scholarship on prophecy and ethics has not entertained. Although worship is important to Israel's life, this study retrieves an ethical vision that is intricately linked to worship to which the texts of the prophets attest. Furthermore, while current scholarship on Old Testament and prophetic ethics does concern itself with the topic of redemption, only Birch hints at the redemption of all creation, a point developed in this study.

Finally, I agree with Janzen that within the biblical story—within the prose and poetry of the prophets—rests an ethic that should be not only retrieved but also assessed. In this way, the biblical text can remain part of a living tradition for a community of believers. Likewise, the writings of the prophets can continue to articulate a vision that is both hopeful and grace-filled as the global community continues to struggle to find new

---

[42]For further discussion, see ibid., 243–307.
[43]Ibid., 251.

ways and expressions of life that are reflective of health, wholeness, and a respect for all creation. This intrinsic goodness and beauty of the Holy is in the midst of all creation, waiting to be discovered amid the ruins of yesterday and the promise of today.

CHAPTER 2

Creation and Covenant

Grounding the Prophets' Ethical Vision in Relationships

The birth of the new millennium has ushered in new discoveries and a "new science" that heralds groundbreaking news: The entire universe is built on relationships. But is this really groundbreaking news? Perhaps it is to twenty-first–century ears, but if one looks back, one will discover that this truth was known intuitively long before it was understood scientifically. Poets of old knew this mystery of the universe. Francis Thompson wrote:

All things by immortal power
near and far
hiddenly
to each other linked are.
Thou canst not stir a flower
without troubling a star.

And if one looks back still further to the Old Testament and reads it anew, one will discover that central to the lives and worldview of the ancient Israelite community was a sense of relationality. This ancient people living in the first millennium understood their God to be the "originator of all things"[1] who shared a "divine relationship to creation."[2]

This God of the biblical text not only shared a divine relationship to creation but also entered into covenant with all creation—the natural

---

[1] Birch, *Let Justice Roll Down*, 72.
[2] Ibid.

world and human beings alike. Covenant established and reflected the formal commitment that God had to creation, and in turn, that human beings would have to their God, to one another, and to the natural world. The ancient biblical people came to understand, then, that covenant was central to life; it sustained life, preserved it, and ensured its future. For them, covenant was relationship—God in relationship with creation, creation in relationship with God; God in relationship with human beings, human beings in relationship with God; human beings in relationship with the natural world, the natural world in relationship with human beings; and God, human beings, and the natural world all in relationship together with all creation, and all creation in relationship with God.[3] Additionally, the ancient biblical people came to understand that to be in covenant was to be interdependent. When covenant was preserved, life flourished. When covenant was broken, life suffered.

The hallmarks of covenant were *mishpat* (justice), *sedeqa* (righteousness), and *hesed* (loving-kindness, mercy). These virtues were later associated with Torah and became part of the prophets' ethical message with its focus on being in right relationship with God and with all of life. Thus, "covenant" and "creation" emerge as two themes central to the biblical text and play a prominent role in the text itself and in the lives of the ancient biblical people.

With respect to the ethics of Israel's prophets, one must first explore the Genesis creation story and the various major covenants in the Old Testament, for within these two topics—with their emphases on "relationships"—lie the cornerstone for and the key to the understanding and evaluation of the prophets' ethical message. The preservation and continuation of right relationships become the reason for and the fruit of an ethical approach to life that flows not from sole obedience and adherence to law, but rather from first being in right relationship with God and all creation. This notion of right relationship rests at the heart of the prophets' message, is central to their vision of a new heaven and a new earth characterized by harmonious relationships, and is the ethical challenge facing the human community today as it struggles to bring *shalom* (peace, wholeness) to birth in this new millennium, this new century that remains pregnant with possibilities amid the burdens of unresolved cares, conflicts, and concerns of times past. If the ethical vision of the prophets is to transcend time, space, and cultures, and if it is to be heard critically and anew in the context of present realities, it must be heard against and in

---

[3]Psalm 104 crystallizes God's care of and relationship to all creation; cf. Psalm 145:15–16; creation's response is one of praise (see, e.g., Psalm 148).

unison with the unfolding drama of creation and the abiding sense of covenant.

Creation: A Vision of Interdependent Relationship

Whether creatures came from stardust or the ground has yet to be determined definitively. And with respect to the theory of creation, whether one espouses the creationist or evolutionist perspective—or something in the middle—has little bearing on what can be gleaned from the Genesis creation story. Clearly, Genesis 1—2 speaks of relationship—a connectedness and unity among that which is divine, human, and nonhuman.

In the priestly creation account (Gen. 1:1—2:4a), God creates in six days the heavens and the earth and all that is within them. God rests on the seventh. This account speaks of several relationships. On the first day God separates "light" and "darkness" from each other; the light God calls "day" and the darkness, "night" (1:3–5). On the second day God establishes a dome in the middle of the waters to separate one body of water from the other (1:6–8). On the third day the water under the sky is gathered into a single basin (the sea) so that the dry land (the earth) may appear (1:9). The earth then brings forth vegetation (1:11–12). On the fourth day, lights—the sun, the moon, and the stars—appear in the dome of the sky to separate day from night (1:14–19). On the fifth day the sea water teems with an abundance of living creatures, and all kinds of birds fly beneath the dome of the sky (1:20–23). On the sixth day the earth brings forth all kinds of living creatures, and God creates human beings—male and female God creates them—who are given the divine task of procreation, which is the same task given to the water creatures and the birds. The human beings are also given the task of caring for the earth and are told to have dominion over earth's creatures (1:24–29). Bruce Birch, Walter Brueggemann, Terrence Fretheim, and David Petersen argue that

> the command to have dominion (1:28), in which God delegates responsibility for the nonhuman creation in power-sharing relationship with humans, must be understood in terms of care-giving, not exploitation (see *radah* in Ps 72:8–14; Ezek 34:1–4). The verb *subdue*, while capable of more negative senses, here has reference to the earth and its cultivation and, more generally, to the becoming of a world that is a dynamic, not a static reality.[4]

---

[4]Bruce C. Birch, Walter Brueggemann, Terence E. Fretheim, and David L. Petersen, *A Theological Introduction to the Old Testament* (Nashville: Abingdon Press, 1999), 50.

God then gives seed-bearing plants and fruit to human beings and green plants to the creatures for their food (1:28–30).

Throughout the priestly creation account, creation is the recipient of divine affirmation: "God saw that it was good" (1:4, 10, 12, 18, 21, 25). When all of creation is completed, God looks at it and finds it "very good" (1:31). Certain elements in creation are the recipients of divine blessing: the sea creatures and birds (1:22), human beings (1:28), and the seventh day (2:3).

Thus, the priestly creation account shows first that there is a relationship between the divine, human, and nonhuman worlds—God is the creator of all, who affirms and blesses creation and who gives certain tasks to some of its members while providing for their sustenance by means of other elements in creation. Second, the things in the created world are ordered in relationship to each other: for example, day and night; the water above the dome and the water below it; the sea and the earth; sea waters teeming with living creatures and skies filled with birds flying; plants and fruit trees and living creatures, both human and nonhuman, which the vegetation nourishes. Even the two great luminaries created on the same day function in relationship to each other and in relation to the day and night. Finally, both human and nonhuman beings are given a common task (to be fertile and multiply), and both share a common foodstock: plants.

In the Yahwistic creation account (Gen. 2:4b–25), one can also detect a relationship that exists among God, the natural world, and humankind. In verse 5 the Yahwistic writer states that no field, shrub, or grass was on the earth because God had sent no rain and there was no person to till the soil. The verse suggests that when God, human beings, and elements in the natural world interact benevolently, life flourishes. In verse 7 one sees that a human being's origin is not only divine but also earthly. God forms a human being out of the dust of the ground and then blows into the being's nostrils, which in turn brings the being to life. Phyllis Trible notes that in Hebrew,

> a play on words already establishes relationship between earth creatures ('adam) and the earth (ha-'adama). This pun is accessible to sight and sound. While uniting creature and soil, it also separates them. *'Adam* is not yet; *ha-'adama* already is. Furthermore, this 'adam is described as potentially acting upon the *'adama* (2:5d).[5]

---

[5]Phyllis Trible, *God and the Rhetoric of Sexuality,* OBT (Philadelphia: Fortress Press, 1978), 77.

In verse 8 God forms a garden in Eden, places the human being in it, and then proceeds to form various trees out of the ground—the same ground used to form the human being. In verse 10 an element in the natural world, a river, rises up to water the garden. In verse 15 God settles the human being in the garden "to till it and keep it."

A contemporary hearing of the charge "to till" and "to keep" illuminates the relationship that exists among all creation:

> "tilling" symbolizes everything we humans do to draw sustenance from nature. It requires individuals to form communities of cooperation and to establish systematic arrangements (economies) for satisfying their needs. Tilling includes not only agriculture but mining and manufacturing and exchanging, all of which depend necessarily on taking and using the stuff of God's creation.[6]

Additionally,

> "keeping" the creation means tilling with care—maintaining the capacity of the creation to provide sustenance for which tilling is done. This, we have come to understand, means making sure that the world of nature may flourish, with all its intricate, interacting systems upon which life depends.[7]

Clearly, the biblical text and interpretation speak of the relationship that exists at the time of creation and that is intrinsic to it. In verse 19, God forms various wild animals and birds of the air out of the ground. In verses 21–22, God forms another human being from the rib of the first one.

Thus, the Yahwistic account shows, as does the priestly creation account, that there is an intricate relationship among all of creation. First, all have a common divine creator, God. Second, all life—vegetation, animals, and human beings—come from *ha-'adama*, the "ground." Third, God, elements in nature, and human effort all help to bring the earth to fruition.

---

[6]From "Restoring Creation for Ecology and Justice," *A Report Adopted by the 202nd General Assembly of the Presbyterian Church (USA)*, Salt Lake City, Utah, 1990, 7.

[7]Ibid. In Trible, *God and the Rhetoric of Sexuality,* 85, the author's comments on "to till" and "to keep" are most insightful. She notes that "to till and to keep, give the earth creature power over the place in which Yahweh God put it." Trible highlights the connection between humanity and botany. She also makes the point that "to till the garden is to serve the garden; to exercise power over it is to reverence it." Finally, she argues that "to till and to keep, connote not plunder and rape but care and attention."

Fourth, human beings are placed and settled in the land and have the divinely ordained task of cultivating and caring for it. And fifth, human beings share in a relationship not only with God and the natural world but also with each other (vv. 21–23).[8]

Together, the priestly and Yahwistic creation accounts show that the relationship between human beings and the natural world, specifically the animals, is a harmonious order based on God's justice and righteousness that overflows into God's care of all creation. Furthermore, both humankind and the animals have a vegetarian diet. Nowhere in Genesis 1—2 is there evidence of any violence or bloodshed on the part of human beings or animals. Nor do human beings hunt or kill animals for food. More to the point, when the human being names the animals (Gen. 2:19–20), a relationship is established, one that, in my opinion, implies bondedness, not dominance. With respect to an ethical attitude toward animals, Jeffrey G. Sobosan offers the following insight:

> The phrase, "the fruits of the earth," [NAB, 1:29] means any plant that grows above or below the ground, and by extension, above or below the water. Of all these Adam and his descendants may eat. But the phrase is also clearly implying a prohibition against consuming animals as food; or differently, it is an injunction toward vegetarianism. Perhaps the motive is the ancient reverence for the spirit in animals; perhaps it is a way for those seeing Adam as the father of the race to distinguish themselves from others (we don't eat meat while the rest of you do); or perhaps it simply represents a dietary aesthetic that found the taste of animal flesh repulsive.
>
> The prohibition, however, may also be expressing the hope for a day when tranquility will prevail between humans and animals and between the animals themselves. It imagines such peace at the beginning of the human story and longs for its eventual resurrection at some future date. This longing is not uncommon in religious and poetic traditions. Isaiah's sweet desire for a time when the lion will lie down with the lamb is not unknown elsewhere; the steady purpose of those who refuse to eat meat is

---

[8]There are many different interpretations of Genesis 2:21–23. While I recognize that, from a feminist perspective, there are certain problems in this verse, namely, that a woman is created from a man's rib, which, in the true sense of things is quite unnatural at best, I choose to stress here that in the context of the entire priestly creation account, verses 21–23 suggest a three-way relationship that exists between God and the first human being, God and the second human being, and the two human beings together.

not recent but has an ancient and honorable lineage. The beauty of this peace has mastered the behavior of many toward animals.[9]

In summary, both the priestly and Yahwistic creation accounts speak of relationships that exist among all aspects of creation in general, and among God, human beings, nonhuman beings, and the natural world in particular. The practice of justice and righteousness maintains these harmonious relationships as proclaimed by Israel's first prophets and becomes the human community's ethical responsibility today, a topic to be discussed in chapter 7.

Covenant: A Commitment to Relationships

Like the creation account in Genesis 1—2, the Noachic, Abrahamic, Sinaitic, and Davidic covenant accounts offer other pictures of the importance of relationships. These four covenants, as well as other "new" covenants, helped to shape the ethical message of Israel's prophets, a message that continues to call the human community to awareness, responsibility, and responsible action today.

The idea of covenant, *berit*, has a long history. Covenants were widespread in the ancient Near Eastern world long before they became part of Israel's way of life. The earliest forms of covenant were political treaties, specifically the Hittite treaties. These were made by a suzerain— a king—with a vassal who, by imposition of the treaty, had to be loyal to the suzerain. This type of suzerain-vassal relationship may or may not have influenced the Old Testament understanding of the covenant that was made between God and Israel.

In the Old Testament are many kinds of covenants.[10] In Exodus, Leviticus, and Numbers, covenant is associated with the giving of the Law.[11] Covenant is a central theological theme in the Old Testament and remains at the heart of Israel's faith, life, and worship. The themes of creation and covenant come together in the story of Noah. The Noachic covenant not only grounds the ethical message of Israel's prophets in the concept of relationship but also becomes part of the prophets' ethical message by way of allusion.[12]

---

[9]Jeffrey G. Sobosan, *Bless the Beasts: A Spirituality for Animal Care* (New York: Crossroad, 1991), 53–54.

[10]For a list of the various ways that *berit* is used, see William L. Holladay, "Covenant God and Covenant People," in *Long Ago God Spoke: How Christians May Hear the Old Testament Today* (Minneapolis: Fortress Press, 1995), 26–39.

[11]See, e.g., Exodus 19:5; 24:7, 8; 31:16; 34:10, 27, 28; Leviticus 24:8; 26:9, 15, 25, 44, 45; Deuteronomy 4:13; 29:1, 21.

[12]See, e.g., Isaiah 24:5; 54:9.

The Noachic Covenant

Bernhard W. Anderson notes that "[the Noachic] covenant was a universal covenant in that it embraced all peoples (the offspring of Noah's sons) and an ecological covenant in that it included the animals and a solemn divine pledge regarding the constancy of 'nature' (Gen. 8:21–22)."[13]

Genesis 9:1–17 describes specifically the covenant that God made with Noah after the idyllic state of Genesis 1—2 had been destroyed by human sin and violence.[14] The biblical text tells us that in response to such chaos, God sent a great flood upon the earth that annihilated everyone and everything (see Gen. 6:11–13 and 7:21–23) except for Noah—a righteous person—his family, and those animals that he took with him into the ark. What is significant here is the fact that humankind had caused sin, violence, and chaos. The flood became a means of divine chastisement of humanity, but unfortunately, the natural world suffered as well. Hence, a systemic connection exists between sin and the suffering of the natural world that will be seen more clearly in the prophetic texts studied in chapter 4.[15]

Verses 8–17 outline the details of the Noachic covenant:

God said to Noah and to his sons with him, "As for me, I am establishing my covenant with you and your descendants after you, and with every living creature that is with you, the birds, the domestic animals, and every animal of the earth with you, as many as came out of the ark. I establish my covenant with you, that never again shall all flesh be cut off by the waters of a flood, and never again shall there be a flood to destroy the earth." God said, "This is the sign of the covenant that I make between me and you and every living creature that is with you, for all future generations: I have set my bow in the clouds, and it shall be a sign of the covenant between me and the earth. When I bring clouds over the earth and the bow is seen in the clouds, I will remember my covenant that is between me and you and every living creature of all flesh; and the waters shall never again become a flood to destroy all flesh. When the bow is in the clouds, I will see it and remember the everlasting covenant between God and every living creature of all flesh that is on the earth." God said to Noah, "This

---

[13]Bernhard W. Anderson, *From Creation to New Creation: Old Testament Perspectives,* OBT (Minneapolis: Fortress Press, 1994), 137.

[14]See, e.g., Genesis 3:1–23; 4:1–16; 6:1–4.

[15]See, e.g., Isaiah 6:8–13; 13:9–13; 24; 33:7–9; 34:8–12; Hosea 4:1–3; Amos 4:6–10; 8:4–8.

is the sign of the covenant that I have established between me and all flesh that is on the earth."

Here one sees that this covenant is not only between God and humanity, namely Noah, his family, and his descendants (v. 9), but also between God and the natural world, specifically the animals (vv. 10, 12) and the earth as a whole (v. 13). Perhaps the most poignant phrase in Genesis 9:1–17 is "I establish my covenant with you, that never again shall all flesh be cut off by the waters of a flood, and never again shall there be a flood to destroy the earth" (9:11). Clearly, the bodily creatures include not only human beings but also the animals, who were innocent victims of God's wrath, all because of human wickedness.[16] The sign of the covenant is a rainbow set in the clouds (vv. 13–14). This covenant is a *berit 'olam,* "an everlasting covenant" that will never be broken on God's part (v. 16). Anderson adds that

> although legal obligations are given in the Noachic covenant, the permanence of the covenant is based on the unconditional commitment of God to the human and nonhuman creation, for better or for worse. In this view, hope for the future does not rest on human performance or improvement, a weak reed on which to lean since human beings do not seem to change, a somber note that was struck in the Old Epic flood tradition (Gen. 8:21) and that reverberates in today's wars and rumors of wars. Rather, hope is based on God's absolute commitment to the creation.[17]

Although there is divine concern for all creatures, and the Noachic covenant extends to the natural world, the picture that Genesis 9:1–17 portrays is not the harmonious relationship between humankind and the animals depicted in the creation accounts. Unlike the creation accounts, the Noachic covenant makes provision for humankind to eat the animals and prohibits only the eating of flesh with its lifeblood still in it (Gen. 9:3–4).

From a contemporary ecological perspective, the issue at stake here is that animals now become part of the food web and aid in the sustenance

---

[16]The portrayal of God as a wrathful God who lashes out against humanity by means of a flood and who gives no consideration to the effects that such chastisement will have on the rest of the natural world is a gruesome picture. One needs to remember that the flood narrative draws on a variety of traditions and is part of Israel's prehistory. In Claus Westermann, *Genesis 1–11, A Commentary,* trans. John J. Scullion (Minneapolis: Augsburg Press, 1984), 395, the author notes that "for the most part the flood narrative occurs as an independent, self-contained story with no sign of the event or occasion that gave rise to it." For further discussion, see Westermann, 393–480.

[17]Anderson, *From Creation to New Creation,* 157–58. For further discussion on the Noachic covenant, see 137–64.

of life for not only human beings but for other animals as well. But the mass slaughter of animals by human beings for profit, the conditions animals are forced to live in prior to their slaughter, and the way in which the slaughter is done are pressing issues that loom large and demand an ethical response. Some developed nations seem to have lost their understanding of interdependence, the reverence for all life, and the spirit of gratitude. Carol S. Robb and Carl J. Casebolt add:

> The [Noachic] covenant is the one that sanctions meat eating. In the context of the relatively wealthy industrialized nations, meat eating is an environmental issue in itself. The food and fiber required for beef raising, for instance, could be distributed widely as protein sources for people who do not have the minimum daily requirements. The same issue affected the people of Palestine, who—with the exception of the wealthy—ate meat only on rare occasions.[18]

In summary, the Noachic covenant is about being in right relationship with creation. The covenant reestablishes the divine–human–nonhuman relationship after it had been breached because of human transgression. This covenant is made with all creation and is "an everlasting covenant." It solidifies the relationship between God and creation for all time and places human beings in relationship with God and the natural world. Thus, when the Israelites transgress the law and break their covenant with God, the natural world suffers. The suffering of the natural world that stems from Israel's transgression of the law and consequent breaching of covenant is a major ethical theme for Israel's prophets. Additionally, the biblical prophetic texts suggest that being in right relationship with God does lead to the actual and promised redemption of humankind and the restoration of the land. Finally, the covenant with Noah provides a foundation for all other covenants and calls the human community today to be in right relationships so that all creation may freely flourish.

The Abrahamic Covenant

Another covenant that speaks of relationships is the Abrahamic covenant (Gen. 15 and 17). Unlike the Noachic covenant, this covenant is made only with Abraham and his descendants, hence, only with human beings and not specifically with the natural world:

---

[18]Carol S. Robb and Carl J. Casebolt, "Introduction," in *Covenant for a New Creation: Ethics, Religion, and Public Policy,* ed. Carol S. Robb and Carl J. Casebolt (Maryknoll, N.Y.: Orbis Books, 1991), 7.

This is my covenant with you: You shall be the ancestor of a multitude of nations. No longer shall your name be Abram, but your name shall be Abraham; for I have made you the ancestor of a multitude of nations...I will make nations of you, and kings shall come from you. I will establish my covenant between me and you, and your offspring after you throughout their generations, for an everlasting covenant [*berit 'olam*], to be God to you and to your offspring after you. (Gen. 17:4–7)

Here, Abraham is promised: (1) descendants, multitudinous and royal; (2) a personal relationship with his God, one that extends to his descendants as well; and (3) perpetuity of the covenant and its promises on the part of God. The divine promises extended to Abraham and his descendants involve another gift—land.

I will give to you, and to your offspring after you, the land where you are now an alien, all the land of Canaan, for a perpetual holding; and I will be their God. (Gen. 17:8)

Like the Noachic covenant, the natural world, specifically the land, plays a key role in the establishment of covenant relationship between God, Abraham, and his descendants. In the Abrahamic covenant, land is one of the gifts promised to the human community at the time when God makes the covenant with Abraham. Although different from the Noachic covenant, the Abrahamic covenant does attest to a human and divine relationship with the natural world as part of it. In this way, these covenants are similar.

The Sinaitic Covenant

One of the most familiar covenants in the Old Testament is the covenant at Sinai that God makes with the Israelite people (Ex. 6:2–8; compare 19:1–9). Mediated through Moses, this covenant formally establishes a relationship between God and Israel: Israel is Yahweh's people and Yahweh is Israel's God. With this covenant comes a series of promises:

Now therefore, if you obey my voice and keep my covenant, you shall be my treasured possession out of all the peoples. Indeed, the whole earth is mine, but you shall be for me a priestly kingdom and a holy nation. (Ex. 19:5–6a)

These promises are contingent on the people's obedience and faithfulness to God. Here and elsewhere in the Old Testament, obedience on the part of the Israelites is to be understood as a means of preserving and remaining in "right relationship" with God and with one another so that they could live securely with abundance in the land (Lev. 25:18; 26:1–13). Implicit, then, in the command to obey God's voice and to keep God's covenant is the assurance of "the good life." Obedience to God's voice implies faithfulness to God's ways made explicit by Torah. And Torah suggests more than following God's Law, which is also given to the Israelites on Sinai in conjunction with the Sinaitic covenant. Torah is an ethical attitude and a way of life, as will be seen in chapter 3. When some of the Israelites are not faithful to God, covenant, and Torah, both the community and the land, as well as the natural world, are made to suffer. The prophets will attribute the cause of this suffering to God, who in wrath chastises the Israelite community because of its transgressions, which violate Torah and break covenant.

Finally, as Robb and Casebolt note, "faithfulness to Yahweh *requires* right relationships among the people."[19] This right relationship among the people has ramifications for the rest of creation, as will be seen in the discussion that follows, which focuses on covenant and the ethical message of Israel's prophets.

The Davidic Covenant

Like the covenants established with Noah and Abraham, the Davidic covenant is a *berit 'olam*, an everlasting covenant: "Your house and your kingdom shall be made sure forever before me; your throne shall be established forever" (2 Sam. 7:16). Mediated by the prophet Nathan to David, this covenant not only offers a series of promises to David but also establishes a multilayered and significant relationship between God and David. In verse 14, Nathan hears God's pledge to David: "I will be a father to him, and he shall be a son to me." This covenant gives divine endorsement to David as king; foreshadows the construction of the temple, which will happen under the leadership of Solomon, David's son and heir apparent; effects a personal relationship between God and David; and guarantees with certitude dynastic succession from the line of David.

Reflecting on the idea of relationship and its connection to the Davidic covenant, Wesley Granberg-Michaelson makes the point that this covenant has far-reaching implications that extend to all creation.

> Seen initially as God's guarantee to rule through the Jerusalem kings in the line of David, this covenant finds affirmation in God's

---

[19]Ibid., 10.

reign over all creation. The justice and righteousness at the foundation of David's throne rests upon God's intention to bring shalom, and right relationships, in all the creation.[20]

In summary, "relationship" rests at the heart of covenant and is the hallmark of creation. Covenant affects creation, and creation is included in covenant. Both creation and covenant, and the relationship that exists between them, play a central role in the ethical message of Israel's prophets.

Covenant, Creation, and Israel's Prophets

The prophetic texts clearly show that the Israelite people had a relationship with creation, specifically with the natural world. For Israel's prophets, images and elements from the natural world become part of their ethical instruction, their messages of impending divine judgment and chastisement, and their oracles of salvation and hope. Natural world imagery forms a basis for the metaphorical language that the prophets employ in order to sting the moral conscience of their listeners or to offer them a vision of comfort. This type of imagery is also used to express the relationship that God and Israel share.

In Jeremiah 5:6, Israel's enemies—described as a lion, a wolf, and a leopard,—lie in wait to attack Israel, which, in the prophetic text, is said to warrant such a harrowing experience because some members of the community are apparently guilty of transgressions and many apostasies. In Ezekiel 19:1–14, the images of a lioness and a vine are used metaphorically to serve the purpose of degrading Israel. Elsewhere, in Ezekiel 34:11–16, the text portrays God's assuming the role of a shepherd, with the Israelites depicted as God's sheep who will be cared for by God because God pities them when they have fallen prey to corrupt leadership and have thus strayed from justice (v. 16). Those sheep whom God will shepherd will be the recipients of God's covenant of peace (v. 25), which God will initiate. Here, images from the natural world converge with the notion of covenant. In Hosea 11:10 God roars "like a lion" only later to become "like the dew" (Hos. 14:5) and "like an evergreen cypress" (Hos. 14:8) for the sake of Israel's salvation.[21]

From these selected examples, one can see that the natural world, which is part of creation, helps to communicate the intent of the prophets'

---

[20]Wesley Granberg-Michaelson, "Covenant and Creation," in *Liberating Life: Contemporary Approaches to Ecological Theology,* ed. Charles Birch, William Eakin, and Jay B. McDaniel (Maryknoll, N.Y.: Orbis Books, 1990), 30.

[21]The prophetic texts are replete with images from the natural world used to express a variety of sentiments. See also Isaiah 5:1–7, 24; 45:8; Jeremiah 5:7–9; Hosea 9:10; 10:11–12; Nahum 3:12, 15b–17; Zechariah 11:1–3.

messages while helping later audiences and readers to see the relationship that the ancient people had with the natural world. This relationship played a major role in their lives as an agrarian people, and it helped to shape and color their imaginations socially, politically, culturally, and theologically.

The connection between creation and covenant emerges most clearly in the prophets' judgment speeches and salvation oracles. Covenant becomes a focal point for the prophets' ethical teaching and preaching. Various biblical texts from the Pentateuch point out that God expected Israel to remain faithful to covenant and the relationships established by covenant.[22]

The prophets heralded this expectation, railed against their people when they broke covenant, and offered them a vision of hope that was contingent on their repentance and God's initiative at making a new covenant with them. From the prophetic texts, one sees that when the Israelites break covenant with God, not only does their relationship with God and with one another suffer but the land and the natural world also suffer.[23] One also sees in the writings of the prophets that when the Israelites repent and return to "right relationship" with their God, social disorder gives way to the promise of the people's redemption (see, e.g., Mic. 4:10 and Am. 3:12) and the restoration of the land and the natural world (see, e.g., Hos. 2:14–23; Joel 2:18–27). As I will suggest in chapter 7, the redemption of humankind is linked to the restoration of the natural world, all of which is the fruit of humankind's being in right relationship with God, which, in turn, leads to humankind's being in right relationship with all creation. As Birch, Brueggemann, Fretheim, and Petersen note,

> the human and the nonhuman orders are deeply integrated, so that human sin has devastating effects on the nonhuman ([Gen.] 3:17; 6:5–7; 9:2). And so the nonhuman creatures are caught up in God's saving work ([Gen.] 6:19—7:3), God's remembering ([Gen.] 8:1), and God's promising ([Gen.] 9:10).[24]

---

[22]See, e.g., Exodus 19:5; Deuteronomy 4:13, 23; 17:2–7; 29:9.

[23]See, e.g., Isaiah 24:4–5; Amos 4:6–12; and Jeremiah 11:1–13. These and other passages will be explored in detail in chapter 4, which gives attention to the suffering of the land and the natural world from historical and contemporary perspectives. A contemporary reading of the biblical texts in relation to the biblical concept of covenant (Charles S. McCoy, "Creation and Covenant: A Comprehensive Vision for Environmental Ethics," in Robb and Casebolt, *Covenant for a New Creation,* 215) states forcefully that "violation of the covenant is an attack upon the created order of the world and is rebellion against God. Injustice, conflict, enmity, and alienation result from unfaithfulness to the covenant; such unfaithfulness disturbs the ordered relation and process of nature, history, and humanity. Actions that violate the covenant do harm to every part of the symbiotically related creation."

[24]Birch, Brueggemann, Fretheim, and Petersen, *A Theological Introduction to the Old Testament,* 45.

Such implications have serious ramifications for the planet today as all creation groans in pain from abuse on the one hand and from anticipation of birth on the other.

The relationship that exists between creation and covenant is apparent in those prophetic texts that deal with a sense of divine judgment. Perturbed by Israel's choice to break covenant through apostasy, idolatry, and lack of faithfulness to Torah, the prophet is featured as one who calls on creation to act as a witness in the divine case being put forth against Israel:

> Hear what the LORD says:
> Rise, plead your case before the mountains,
> and let the hills hear your voice.
> Hear, you mountains, the controversy of the LORD,
> and you enduring foundations of the earth;
> for the LORD has a controversy with his people,
> and he will contend with Israel. (Mic. 6:1–2)

These verses are a classic example of a *rîb,* a covenant "lawsuit." God's specific case against Israel follows in Micah 6:3–5. Another example similar to Micah 6:1–2 occurs in Isaiah 34:1–2:

> Draw near, O nations, to hear;
> O peoples, give heed!
> Let the earth hear, and all that fills it;
> the world, and all that comes from it.
> For the LORD is enraged against all the nations,
> and furious against all their hordes;
> he has doomed them, has given them over for slaughter.

What unfolds in the later verses of this judgment oracle is a gruesome vision of God's intended punitive chastisement (vv. 3–15). In support of this notion of creation's acting as a witness on God's behalf, Ronald A. Simkins asserts that "in the biblical tradition there are no other gods to witness God's covenant with Israel. Thus, creation stands as a testimony and witness of God's commitment to the people and of the people's oath to be faithful to God."[25]

Clearly, the message of Israel's prophets, along with those selected pentateuchal passages that speak of creation and covenant, attest to an intricate relationship that existed between creation and covenant in the

---

[25]Ronald A. Simkins, *Creator and Creation* (Peabody, Mass.: Hendrickson, 1994), 159.

ancient world.[26] This relationship continues to exist in this new century and millennium in which we struggle with socioecological injustices because, as in the days of ancient Israel, some members of the human community are not in right relationship with one another and with the natural world. Hence, all creation feels the pain of injustice that results in cosmic depravity and brokenness. This link between creation and covenant and the prophetic call to be in right relationship is central to the ethical message of Israel's prophets; it becomes the foundation for a new prophetic ethic that must be universal if it is to respond to the needs of and have an effect on the planet as a whole.

Finally, in order to preserve right relationships with God, humanity, and all creation, as covenant tries to do, Israel is entrusted with Torah, God's Law, which calls the people to an ethical way of life. Hence, Torah becomes a means to an end, and that end is wholeness and preservation of one's relationship with God, one's relationship with creation, and creation itself, not because it is useful but because it is "good"; it is "very good."[27]

---

[26]McCoy, "Creation and Covenant" sums up the idea of the relatedness of creation and covenant in his comment that "covenant reaches back to creation and depicts the origin of the world in God's faithful action. Covenant points forward toward the consummation of the process initiated in creation. The wholeness of creation, coming to focus in the coherent pattern and responsibility of everyone present, is covenantal, is faithful. Nature no less than history is understood through covenant. The covenant of the rainbow after the flood reminds us of the inclusion of nature" (215).

[27]See Genesis 1:4, 10, 12, 18, 21, 25, and 31, respectively.

CHAPTER 3

Torah

An Attitude and Way of Life That Inform the Ethics of Israel's Prophets

Central to the preservation of covenant and right relationship with all creation is Torah. Torah also contributes to the ethical vision of the prophets. Although it is often understood as "law," Torah as a concept is much broader. James A. Sanders points out that the "oldest and most common meaning" of Torah appears to be "something approximate to what we mean by the word *revelation*. Priestly and prophetic oracles of the oldest vintage are called torahs."[1] Sanders notes further that the word *torah* is derived from a Semitic root that means "to cast" or "to throw."

Torah also comes to be understood as "instruction"[2] that takes the form of a teaching. Those who teach Torah include priests, prophets, sages, and parents of children.[3] Torah's didactic form makes the concept more closely related to narrative and story rather than law codes or a series of

---

[1] For further discussion, see James A. Sanders, *Torah and Canon* (Philadelphia: Fortress Press, 1972), 2.

[2] Ibid., 1.

[3] See Frank Crüsemann, *The Torah: Theology and Social History of the Old Testament Law,* trans. Allan W. Mahnke (Minneapolis: Fortress Press, 1996), 2. On the point of Torah as "instruction" and priests, prophets, sages, and parents as teachers of Torah, Crüsemann notes that "the word Torah in the everyday speech of the Old Testament meant instructions given by a mother (Prov. 1:8, 6:20, cf. 31:26) and a father (4:1f) to their children to instruct them in matters of living and to warn them about mortally dangerous situations. In its early function as well as later uses, the word implies information, advice, instruction, the establishment of norms, demand as well as encouragement, command but also benefits. The concept of Torah became a technical term for priestly instruction to the laity (Jer. 18:18; Ezra 7:25), but it also designates speech of the wisdom teachers (Prov. 7:2 ; 13:14) or the prophets (Isa. 8:16, 20; 30:9) to pupils."

legal standards, but this does not negate the fact that the instruction—the narrative, the story—often has an ethical dimension or message.

In the period of the late Old Testament in Judaism, Torah par excellence is applied to the first books of the Bible, otherwise known as the Pentateuch, the Book of the Law, or simply the Torah. As an instruction with an ethical dimension—and thus a legal sense—to it, Torah becomes understood as something related to law, but it can never be identified as law alone because of its link to covenant and the relationships that undergird it. Byron L. Sherwin states the point forthrightly:

> As a *contract*, the Torah is a legal document which states the mutually accepted duties and responsibilities of the two parties [God and Israel] to the agreement. However as a *marriage* contract, the Torah is a document which attests to the love…between God and Israel. Thus, while it embodies a legal element, the Torah is not simply law; rather, it embraces a polarity of love *and* law.[4]

Hence, as a document produced "*in a community of faith for the instruction of communities of faith*,"[5] Torah is "given for guidance, so that Israel (and all of Israel's belated heirs) are 'clued in' to the defining expectations of the relationship,"[6] namely, the relationship that exists between God and Israel.

As an expression of a way of life that incorporates an ethical system, Torah is intended to establish and preserve not only relationships but also "the good life," which is the blessing of "right relationship":

> You shall observe my statutes and faithfully keep my ordinances, so that you may live on the land securely. The land will yield its fruit, and you will eat your fill and live on it securely. (Lev. 25: 18–19)

Torah, then, implies observance of and adherence to certain ethical norms. These ethical norms become part of the fabric of Israel's life and are embedded in Israel's history and story.

The observance of and adherence to the ethical norms embedded in Israel's life, history, and story is never meant to be a blind and legalistic obedience. Faithfulness to an ethical way of life as prescribed by Torah is always for the purpose of safeguarding relationships: God's relationship with Israel, Israel's relationship with God, God's and Israel's relationship

---

[4]Byron L. Sherwin, "Law and Love in Jewish Theology," *ATR* 64 (19): 468; cf. Birch, *Let Justice Roll Down*, 171.

[5]John Andrew Dearman, "The Blessing of Torah: Preaching the Gospel Beforehand," *Austin Seminary Bulletin: Faculty Edition* (1990), 35.

[6]Walter Brueggemann, *The Covenanted Self: Explorations in Law and Covenant* (Minneapolis: Fortress Press, 1999), 37.

with other peoples, and God's and Israel's relationship with all creation. Calling to mind Leviticus 26, which outlines the rewards that come with faithfulness to Torah and its ethical aspects as they are related to covenant (see Lev. 26:14–15), as well as the consequences that result from a lack of faithfulness, Bruce Birch, Walter Brueggemann, Terence E. Fretheim, and David L. Petersen stress that

> Israel's law, as with ancient Near Eastern law generally, is most fundamentally associated with creation. This may be observed in the symbolic relationship between social orders. Negatively, disobedience of law has adverse effects in both natural and sociopolitical realms (e.g., Lev. 26:19–22, 31–34); positively, obedience is a means by which the divine ordering in creation can be actualized in these same spheres (26:4–10). As such, the law is understood basically in vocational terms. That is, it is grounded in God's work in creation and serves God's purposes of life, stability, and the flourishing of individuals and communities. To this vocation Israel is called, for the sake of creation.
>
> God's creation has been disrupted by sin and its effects; the divine objective in both redemption and law is the reclamation of creation. In attending to the law, Israel joins God in seeking to keep right what God has put in redemption, and to extend that rightness into every sphere of life. To that end, God's redemptive work empowers Israel in its vocation and provides paradigms and motivations for obedience...[7]

Thus, Torah as a way of life flows from and is supportive of a covenant relationship that includes all creation.

Finally, Torah can no longer be understood anthropocentrically. With its cosmological scope now retrieved, it is incumbent on the believing community today to realize that particular attitude toward life, one that speaks of a reverence and respect for all creation and that finds its expression in an ethical way of life that is both social and ecological. Such an attitude and expressed way of life become a testimony to the divine vision that all creation is intrinsically "good," "very good,"[8] and destined for restoration and redemption.[9]

---

[7] Birch, Brueggemann, Fretheim, and Petersen, *A Theological Introduction to the Old Testament,* 158.

[8] See Genesis 1—2.

[9] See, e.g., Isaiah 11; 61:1–4; 65:17–25; Micah 4:1–4; Joel 2:21–22; Matthew 12:15–21; Luke 2:29–38; 4:16–21; Romans 8:18–25; Colossians 1:15–20. These texts individually and collectively speak about the restoration of both the natural world and the redemption of humanity and creation. The link between the restoration of creation and the redemption of humanity is explored further in chapter 6.

Ethical Aspects of Israelite Law

Integral to Torah as an attitude and way of life is the concept of law. As part of Torah, law is meant not only to preserve and safeguard covenant and those relationships that are part of covenant but also to call people to an ethical way of life that acknowledges and celebrates the intrinsic goodness of all creation. The four law codes, the individual laws within these codes, as well as the Decalogue, all of which are embedded in Israel's history and story, bespeak a care and concern for all creation and the preservation of covenant relationship. These codes with their respective laws and the Decalogue help to share the prophets' ethical message, which casts judgment, but not without a vision of hope and salvation.

The Covenant Code

The Covenant Code, one of Israel's oldest legal collections, begins in Exodus 20:22 and continues through to Exodus 23:19. Following verse 19 is a series of promises and exhortations (vv. 20–33) aimed at encouraging the Israelites to remain faithful to God and God's ways in the midst of their being surrounded by diverse peoples who engage in cultic practices not acceptable to Israel's God.

Small blocks of various individual laws compose the Covenant Code. For example, Exodus 20:22–26 outlines the kind of altar that is acceptable to God and the types of sacrifices to be offered upon it. Exodus 21:1–11 gives laws concerning slaves; Exodus 21:12–27 focuses on violence and outlines what could be considered capital crimes and their penalties (vv. 12–17) and those lesser crimes that involve injury to other people but do not warrant death as a penalty (vv. 18–27). Exodus 21:28–36 descriies laws that safeguard property, while Exodus 22:1–15 highlights laws of restitution. Those laws that pertain to other social and religious aspects of life appear in Exodus 22:16–31. Highlighted in these laws is a concern for the resident alien (v. 21), the widowed and fatherless (v. 22), and the poor (v. 25). Exodus 23:1–9 provides an all-encompassing view of law that safeguards not only truth but also animals and people, especially the poor (v. 6) and the resident alien (v. 9). Added to this list of laws that protect animals and people are laws that govern rest, an experience to be enjoyed not only by people and animals but the land itself as well (Ex. 23:10–13). Finally, Exodus 23:14–19 offers an instruction on how to celebrate the annual festivals, with verse 19b being a concluding prohibition that expresses care for a young animal: "You shall not boil a kid in its mother's milk."

All these blocks of laws within the Covenant Code are concerned with the appropriate care and respect that is to be given to God, people, and the natural world. Hence, Israel's justice has a social as well as an ecological perspective that reflects an understanding of relationship and covenant. This understanding of relationship and covenant includes human, nonhuman, and divine life, and, as mentioned in chapter 2, it begins with the Genesis creation account[10] and the story of Noah.[11] Many of the laws contained within the Covenant Code are alluded to in the ethical message and vision of the prophets.

The Deuteronomic Code

Like the Covenant Code, the Deuteronomic Code plays a major role in Israel's life as a community and its relationship with God and creation. Couched in the book of Deuteronomy and woven into the fibers of Israel's life story, those laws that compose the Deuteronomic Code are found in Deuteronomy 12—26, and perhaps in 28:1–6, 16–19.[12] Included in this law code are laws governing cult and religion (Deut. 12:2—17:7); laws pertaining to the establishment of various legal officials, offices, decisions, and other institutions (Deut. 16:18–20; 17:8—20:20); and laws focusing on social justice (Deut. 21:1—25:19). The last part of the Deuteronomic Code is an instruction on ritual practice (26:1–15) and an exhortation. This concern for social justice is a feature throughout the Deuteronomic Code, and, as in the Covenant Code, attention is drawn to resident aliens (Deut. 14:21, 29; 24:14–22), widows, and the fatherless (Deut. 14:29; 16:11, 14). Additionally, the Deuteronomic Code offers instruction on social justice for slaves and laborers (Deut. 15:12–18; 24:7, 14–15) as well. Furthermore, this law code aims at establishing "fair and equitable procedures in the administration of justice."[13] The various laws and instructions contained in the Deuteronomic Code resonate in the ethical message and vision of Israel's prophets, as will be highlighted at the end of this chapter and explored in the next.

---

[10]See Genesis 1—2, especially 2:7, 18–23. Also note that according to the Genesis creation account, human beings, the plants, and the animals are formed from "the ground," the woman, who is said to have been formed from the man's rib, being the exception in the story (v. 22). Hence, a relationship is established between human and nonhuman life and includes the divine as well: Both the animals and human beings are the recipients of God's blessing (Gen. 1:22, 28).

[11]See Genesis 9:1–17.

[12]See William L. Holladay, *Long Ago God Spoke: How Christians May Hear the Old Testament Today* (Minneapolis: Fortress Press, 1995), 43. Holladay notes that the material of the Deuteronomic Code "seems to have been influenced by the early prophets, particularly Hosea in the eighth century B.C.E." (43).

[13]Edward McGlynn Gaffney, Jr., "Of Covenants Ancient and New: The Influence of Secular Law on Biblical Religion," *JLR* 2 (1984): 131. Gaffney asserts further that within the Deuteronomic Code specific material attests to the existence of equity that governed the administration of justice: "Commercial reforms include statutes aimed at the maintenance of fair business practices (Deut. 25:13–16); at elimination of usury and abusive debt collection (Deut. 23;19ff.; 24:6, 10–13, 17); and at the forgiveness of unmanageable debt on a regular basis, but with safeguards against abuse (Deut. 15:1–11)" (131).

The Holiness Code

Located in Leviticus 17—26, the Holiness Code's main theme is holiness. Israel must be holy because God is holy (Lev. 19:2). This code suggests that the Israelites heed certain instructions and adhere to various laws so that the divine charge "to be holy" might be evidenced in and through their lives. Leviticus 17:1–9 is an instruction on animal slaughter for the purpose of sacrifice. Leviticus 17:10–16 focuses on the prohibition against eating blood. Chapters 18—20 describe the type of personal conduct befitting Israelites as a holy people. Specified in these chapters are laws for sexual relations (18:2–30), laws and guidelines for maintaining ritual and moral holiness (19:2–37), and a list that outlines various consequences the Israelites would experience if they violated the Holiness Code in general and those laws that prohibit certain cultic and sexual activities in particular. Leviticus 21:2–24 contains a series of laws directed at Israel's priests. An instruction on the use of holy offerings and what offerings are considered acceptable to God is the topic of Leviticus 22. Leviticus 23:1—24:9 highlights certain festivals and rituals and outlines how these celebrations are to be conducted. Those who blaspheme or take a person's or animal's life without due cause will be punished as outlined in Leviticus 24:10–23. Leviticus 25 offers a detailed description of laws and instructions that are to govern the sabbatical and jubilee years. And finally, Leviticus 26 lists the rewards for obedience (vv. 1–13) and the penalties for disobedience (vv. 14–45). The code closes with a summary statement: "These are the statutes and ordinances and laws that the LORD established between himself and the people of Israel on Mount Sinai through Moses" (Lev. 26:46).

Like the Covenant and Deuteronomic Codes, the Holiness Code emphasizes what the Israelites need to do to continue in "right relationship" with God and with one another. All three of these codes aim at the preservation of "covenant," the special bond that the people have with God, with one another, and with creation. In particular, the Holiness Code prescribes laws and instructions that include the natural world. In this way, this code is similar to the Deuteronomic Code. Thus, these two codes contain not only a social dimension but an ecological one as well. The Holiness Code, like the other two codes discussed thus far, figures in the ethical message and vision of Israel's prophets, a topic that is explored in chapter 4.

The Priestly Code

Unlike the other three law codes, the so-called Priestly Code cannot be confined to one specific book. Exodus 12:1–20, 12:40–50, 35:1–3; Leviticus 1—16, 27; and Numbers 1—10, 15, 18—19, 27—30 all contain material proper to the Priestly Code. The book of Exodus presents a variety of instructions and laws that concern the First Passover (12:1–20, 40–50) and Sabbath rest (35:1–3).

The book of Leviticus offers teachings and laws that pertain to offerings and sacrifices (chaps. 1—7), the rites of ordination (chap. 8), and a description of the inauguration of Aaron's priesthood (chap. 9), followed by a story about Aaron's two sons, Nadab and Abihu (chap. 10). Additional instructions and laws focus on clean and unclean food (11:1–23); unclean animals (11:24–47); the purification of women after childbirth (chap. 12); symptoms, care for, and precautions concerning leprosy (chaps. 13—14); male and female bodily discharges (chap. 15); the Day of Atonement (chap. 16); and votive offerings (chap. 27).

The book of Numbers features instructions and laws concerning the first census of Israel (chaps. 1—4), in which the duties of the Levite priests (3:5–13) and a comment on the redemption of the firstborn (3:40–51) are couched. Also included in this section of the Priestly Code are further instructions and laws relative to unclean persons (5:1–4); confession and restitution (5:5–10); an unfaithful wife (5:11–31); the Nazirites (chap. 6); the offerings of the Israelite leaders (chap. 7); the setting up of the seven lamps (8:1–4); the consecration and service of the Levites (8:5–26); the celebration of the Passover at Sinai (9:1–14); and the construction and sounding of the two silver trumpets (10:1–10). Within this body of material is the description of how Moses is to bless the people (6:22–27), a lesson about the cloud and the fire and the Israelites' response to it (9:15–23), and a catalog of events highlighting the Israelites' departure from Sinai (10:11–36). Numbers 15:2–31 gives instruction on various offerings accompanied by detailed descriptions of what God requires of the Israelites with respect to the offerings. Also included in Numbers 15 is a story about how, at God's command, the Israelites stoned to death a man who violated the Sabbath (vv. 32–36). An instruction on how to make fringes on a garment and the purpose of such an exercise (vv. 37–41) follows the Sabbath story. Numbers 18 focuses on matters exclusive to the priests and Levites, followed by various instructions and laws concerning purification rituals (Num. 19) that were pertinent to the entire Israelite community. Finally, the last four chapters of Numbers to be included in the Priestly Code are chapters 27—30. These chapters center on instructions and laws related to inheritances (27:1–11); the appointment of Joshua as Moses' successor (27:12–23); various offerings (chaps. 28—29); and vows made by women (chap. 30).

Clearly, the Priestly Code focuses on religious and cultic matters within the Israelite community. Unlike the three other law codes, the Priestly Code does not have a strong emphasis on social justice, but it does stress the responsibilities that the priests and Levites have in service to God and to the people. Similar to the other codes, this one does stress the importance of being in right relationship with one another and especially with God. The mention of the Sabbath in the Priestly Code (Ex. 35:1–3 and Num. 15:32–36) recalls the instructions and laws pertaining to the Sabbath and Sabbatical year as put forth by the Covenant, Deuteronomic, and Holiness Codes (see Ex. 23:10–13; Deut. 15:1–18; and Lev. 25:1–7, respectively). These references to rest link not only the Priestly Code but the other three law codes as well to the Genesis creation account (Gen. 2:1–3). Hence, creation, right relationships, and law are all in some way connected and help to flesh out, preserve, and maintain the covenant relationship that Israel shares with God and with all creation, and vice versa. As will be seen in chapter 4, the prophets do hold the people accountable to an unqualified relationship with their God as well as the faithful living out of God's ways mirrored in the four law codes. The responsibilities of the priest and the types of offerings to be made by the people to God, all outlined by the Priestly Code, have a particular emphasis in the prophets' ethical message and vision.

The Decalogue

Popularly called the Ten Commandments, the Decalogue appears in Exodus 20:2–17 and Deuteronomy 5:6–21. In the Exodus rendition— the focus of this section—God talks to the Israelites directly, and personally gives them the Decalogue on Mount Sinai. In the Deuteronomy rendition the Israelites receive the Decalogue through Moses, who speaks to them in a homily on the plains of Moab. Although there are differences between the two renditions, both "promote and protect the life and well-being of the *community*."[14]

As a sign of the Sinaitic Covenant (Ex. 6:2–8), the Decalogue given on Mount Sinai lays down the stipulations of the covenant. Thus, the Israelite people are the recipients of God's covenant as well as God's law. Exodus 20:2–17 can be divided into three blocks of material: verses 2–7, 8–11, and 12–17.

Verses 2–7 focus on being in right relationship with God. These verses call the Israelites to covenant fidelity and challenge them to remember who their God is. The verses speak of God's sovereignty and power and warn the Israelites indirectly against the pitfalls and consequences of idolatry.

---

[14]Birch, Brueggemann, Fretheim, and Petersen, *A Theological Introduction to the Old Testament*, 132.

The verses exhort them not to make wrongful use of the divine name, which, if they did, would result in the loss of divine favor.

Verses 8–11 are an exhortation to remember and to keep holy the sabbath day. These verses imply Sabbath rest and make clear that this experience is to be enjoyed by all people, regardless of their status, together with the natural world, and here specifically, the animals. This reference to a day of rest harks back to the creation account (Gen. 2:1–3) and echoes similar proscriptions found in the other law codes (compare Ex. 23:10–13; Lev. 25:1–7; Deut. 15:1–18).

Central to the concept of Sabbath is the idea of the mutual relationship shared between God and creation. Dearman points out that

> the Sabbath is a day prepared for the people of God whereby rest reminds them of God's blessing and confirms their place in it. Their honoring of the Sabbath day "to keep it holy" becomes a means by which they, in turn, bless God. The blessing of the seventh day, when read in the context of worship, provides another important element of blessing. It is supremely a relational term; not only can God bless elements of creation or the human species, they bless God.[15]

Continuing Dearman's notion of relationality, Susan Niditch adds:

> The centerpiece of the little code in Exodus 20 involves the Sabbath, an important demarcator of the week's experience that invokes the closure of the creation process. Israelites are required to encode the rhythm of their weeks with the pattern of Yahweh's work as world creator. The Sabbath thus becomes an important symbolic link between the divine/human relationship and the human way of life, which is further addressed in verses 12–17.[16]

Verses 12–17 are a series of laws aimed at preserving and maintaining right relationships with family members and with other members of the human community. With the command to honor one's father and mother in verse 12a comes another glimpse of "the good life" mentioned in Leviticus 25:18. According to verse 12, respect for one's parents is intricately connected to one's future enjoyment of a long life to be lived in the land that God is about to give as a gift. With respect to verses 12–17, Brueggemann observes that

---

[15]Dearman, "The Blessing of Torah," 39–40.
[16]Susan Niditch, *Ancient Israelite Religion* (New York: Oxford University Press, 1997), 73.

the fifth through tenth Commandments are assertions about the kind of caring neighborliness that ensures that a community of covenant will not degenerate into a society of abuse, disrespect, oppression, and finally, brutality. The commandments are a line drawn against brutality. They insist that people do not *earn* standing in this community but are *entitled* to an honorable place simply because they belong in the community.[17]

In summary, the Decalogue given on Mount Sinai has as its main theme right relationships, inclusive of God, the human community, and the natural world. The Decalogue as a series of laws has as its intent the safeguarding and living out of the covenant. Integral to the Decalogue is the remembrance of the sabbath day and the rest that it is meant to bring to creation. Thus, the Decalogue draws on themes associated with creation and covenant, and shows how law is meant to incorporate and sustain both, with all in the embrace of God. The Decalogue, along with the other law codes, helps to form the ethical backbone of the prophets' message and vision.

Justice, Righteousness, and Steadfast Love

One cannot talk about the ethics of Israel's prophets without first considering the hallmarks of covenant, namely, *mishpat* (justice), *sedeqa* (righteousness), and *hesed* (steadfast love),[18] all of which lead to an ethical way of life that encompasses creation, covenant, and Torah, and which nurtures, sustains, and gives birth to right relationships amid every aspect of life. God's holiness and steadfast love are expressed in myriad ways throughout the Bible, but in the Old Testament these divine attributes are especially recognizable in and through covenant relationship. As Birch notes, "Covenant relationship is the framework within which Israel apprehends and relates to God's demands for justice and righteousness…"[19] Furthermore, "Israel's life as a concrete social reality is to reflect the qualities already modeled by God in Israel's experience. Righteousness and justice are the terms most often used to characterize what is called for in covenant society."[20]

---

[17]Walter Brueggemann, *Interpretation and Obedience* (Minneapolis: Fortress Press, 1991), 149.

[18]The word *hesed* can be understood in a variety of ways, such as "loyalty," "loving-kindness," or "steadfast love." I have translated it as "steadfast love," in keeping with the English version of the NRSV.

[19]Birch, *Let Justice Roll Down,* 156.

[20]Ibid., 177.

In addition to justice and righteousness as divine attributes and characteristics of a covenant society, steadfast love is an essential quality of the relationship that God has with the Israelite community, and, in essence, with all creation (see, e.g., Ps. 136; also compare Ps. 104:1–30). God's steadfast love "points to God's actions of loving fidelity to the covenant relationship."[21] Such actions, in turn, must become a quality of all relationships that humankind shares with the living and nonliving world, since God's covenant and steadfast love embrace all creation, beginning with the creation story and the covenant made with Noah.

Throughout the Old Testament, justice, righteousness, and steadfast love play a major role in the lives and good choices (or lack thereof) of the human community in general, and the Israelite community in particular.[22] Nowhere, however, do these virtues appear with such force, directness, and promise as they do in the books of the prophets and in their ethical message. For example, justice is what the Israelite community fails to practice in its dealings with one another (see, e.g., Mic. 3:1–3). But all hope is not lost. On the day when God will make a new covenant with Israel, one that will include the natural world (see Hos. 2:16–18), God will espouse Israel in righteousness, justice, and steadfast love (Hos. 2:19).

God, creation, covenant, Torah, justice, righteousness, steadfast love, and the relationships engendered and sustained by all these dimensions and attitudes toward life are what bring Israel's prophets' ethical message and vision to a crescendo. The message and vision have yet to reach their final note in this present time, when we continue to look for hope amid the ruins of yesterdays past.

---

[21] Ibid., 153.

[22] For a comprehensive study of justice, righteousness, and steadfast love, see Gossai, *Justice, Righteousness, and the Social Critique of the Eighth-Century Prophets.*

CHAPTER 4

The Prophetic Voice

Exposing the Obvious and Unmasking the Implied

Israel's prophets are perhaps best viewed not as moralists or idealists but as poets, storytellers, and preachers who, because of their great love of God and of all creation, are willing—however reluctantly—to proclaim an unpopular yet steadfast love. Concerned not only with advocating a quality of life that finds expression in and through right relationships with both human and nonhuman life, the prophets continually remind people of the wholeness and holiness of all creation, and the effects that human sin has on it.

Double-visioned and single-hearted, Israel's prophets see life as it truly is with all its beauty and sham, and challenge people again and again to come to grips with and embrace the unfolding and mysterious plan of universal salvation for all creation. Their ethical message, camouflaged in images representative of their life experience, cuts to the chase to sting people with its moral consciousness and to call them to responsibility. It also helps them to envision intuitively and imaginatively what life will be like at the time of the new heavens and the new earth that are already being created in the here and now.

Heard in the context of contemporary times, the message of Israel's prophets is time-conditioned yet timeless. Having social and ecological implications for a present-day people and planet that grope for signs of hope as both struggle to give birth to the envisioned new order, the prophets' ethical message, as challenging and hopeful as it is, cannot go unquestioned or unchallenged. How ethical is the message of Israel's prophets? This question remains central to the following discussion, which seeks not only to present the prophets' ethical message but also to evaluate its ethics from a contemporary hermeneutical perspective.

Apostasy and Idolatry

Two of Israel's main transgressions are apostasy and idolatry, with apostasy often resulting in idolatry. Forgetfulness of Yahweh leads to forgetfulness of Yahweh's ways, which results in political, social, economic, and religious corruption and chaos that ends in the destruction of both the Northern Kingdom Israel in 721 B.C.E. and the Southern Kingdom Judah, along with the holy city Jerusalem and the temple, in 587 B.C.E. Isaiah, Jeremiah, Ezekiel, Hosea, and Micah all address the problem of apostasy that exists within the Israelite community.

Isaiah 1:2–9

Cosmological in its focus, this judgment speech opens with a double summons and two apostrophes aimed at calling creation to witness the divine word about to be proclaimed to Judah[1]:

Hear, O heavens, and listen, O earth;
for the LORD has spoken: (1:2)

Yahweh's judgment of the apostate Israelites follows in 1:1b–8. Images from the natural world (vv. 3, 7–8) serve to emphasize the nation's ignorance (v. 3) and its grim future (vv. 7–8). A comment by the prophet in verse 9 closes the passage and sheds light on God's mercy. Verse 4 highlights the Israelites' transgressions:

Ah, sinful nation,
people laden with iniquity,
offspring who do evil,
children who deal corruptly,
who have forsaken the LORD,
who have despised the Holy One of Israel,
who are utterly estranged! (1:4)

A chosen people, once distinct and holy, Israel is now a sinful nation full of corruption. Such a condition stems from Israel's apostasy. Clearly, the text attests to a breach in covenant relationship with God: Israel has forsaken and despised the Holy One. Israel has fallen out of right

---

[1]Summoning the heavens and earth is a common motif in the Old Testament. See, e.g., Deuteronomy 4:26; Psalm 50:4–5; Jeremiah 2:12.

relationship with God, and in so doing has abandoned God's ways, only to sink into the mire of iniquity. Israel has become utterly estranged. Foreshadowed by Deuteronomy 31:16, Israel's sad state warrants divine chastisement (see Deut. 28:20), and indeed, the nation will receive it (Isa. 1:7–8). Judah is doomed to destruction, and such action will be attributed to God.[2]

As a whole, the text reflects a theological belief popular in the ancient world, namely, the deuteronomistic theology of retribution. According to this theological construct, if one is obedient to God's word and ways, God will reward that person, whereas disobedience brings punishment (see, e.g., Deut. 28). Thus, because Israel forsakes God and breaches the covenant relationship, Israel is to experience God's wrath (vv. 5–8). Note that the biblical text in general, as well as the oral tradition that underlies it, is culturally conditioned. This prophetic message and text are no exception. One also wonders, then, if the author and final editor of this prophetic text shared a similar theological understanding and worldview with the prophet? Finally, the notion of corporate responsibility is not uncommon in the ancient world. If a few Israelites were guilty of an offense, all were deserving of divine chastisement.[3] Only through God's mercy would some be spared. Again, popular beliefs of the day colored the theological understanding of the prophets and influenced their messages and the written texts that flowed from their oral tradition. One wonders, then, if the entire nation was as sinful as the text would have us think. Furthermore, how ethical would it be today to chastise a whole group for the transgressions of a few?

In summary, the initial transgression of apostasy placed God and the Israelites in the fray. This situation negatively affects all of Israel's other relationships. This lack of right relationship with God carries consequences not only for people but also for the natural world (see v. 7). Hence, creation suffers when there is a breach in covenant relationship, especially a breach between human beings and God or between human beings.

Jeremiah 5:1–17

A further description of Israel's apostate and iniquitous state occurs in Jeremiah 5:1–11. In verses 1–2, God challenges the prophet and indicts

---

[2]The verbs in verses 7–8 are present tense not because the events of desolation have in fact happened but to assure the people that, indeed, these events will happen. In prophetic literature the use of past and present tenses to describe a pending action in such a way as to suggest that the action has already happened is common and functions to assure the prophet's original hearers and later (re)readers of the text that indeed the event will take place.

[3]For further discussion, see Joel S. Kaminsky, *Corporate Responsibility in the Hebrew Bible,* JSOTSup 196 (Sheffield, England: Sheffield Academic Press, 1995).

the Israelites. God offers Jeremiah the task of finding among the Israelites one person who acts justly and seeks the truth. God's stated intention is to pardon Jerusalem if the prophet is able to find one such righteous person (v. 1). In verse 2, God reveals the double-standard at the heart of Israel's life. It seems that the people do not speak truthfully in the name of God. Thus, the expressed desire to forgive appears to be tongue-in-cheek on God's part, which the prophet seems not to catch on to at first, since he responds to the divine challenge with a rhetorical question that points up his bewilderment at God's perception of the present situation: "O LORD, do your eyes not look for truth?" (v. 3). The prophet next recalls for God all the things God has done to chastise the people for their injustices and this lack of truthfulness and then reminds God of the people's bold arrogance and stubbornness:

> They have made their faces harder than rock;
> They have refused to turn back. (v. 3)

Indirectly, the prophet himself indicts the Israelite community before God.

Verses 4–6 depict the prophet's embracing God's challenge, which was stated in verses 1–2. Not expecting to find anyone among the poor who would be righteous because "they have no sense" and "they do not know the way of the LORD" nor "the law of their God" (v. 4), he moves on to consider the rich, assuming that they are cognizant of God and God's ways, but he soon discovers that like the poor, they too "had broken the yoke" and "had burst the bonds" (v. 5). The prophet finds no one in the community who is just and truthful and concludes that because of their many transgressions and great apostasies, they will be made to suffer terrible consequences (v. 6). Thus, verse 6 describes what the prophet comes to realize will be Israel's lot and also serves as an announcement of an impending disaster that will befall the community because of its waywardness.[4]

With the prophet's original sense of the nation confirmed (v. 3), God now continues the dialogue (vv. 7–9). Responding to the prophet's experience and indirect indictment of the community, God confronts the prophet with a rhetorical question (v. 7): "How can I pardon you?" William L. Holladay points out that "the rhetorical question echoes the last colon of v 1 and by its form implies the near-impossibility of pardon."[5] Just as

---

[4]As is seen further in Jeremiah 5, this disaster will take the form of an invading army that will destroy the nation Israel. Such action will be understood by the prophet—and eventually by the people—as something that God executes in order to punish the nation because of its transgressions (see 5:14–17).

[5]William L. Holladay, *Jeremiah 1,* Hermeneia (Philadelphia: Fortress Press, 1986), 179.

the prophet confronted God in verse 3, so now God confronts the prophet. Following the rhetorical question, God exposes the people's transgressions: They are guilty of apostasy and idolatry, which are interrelated through the metaphorical reference to adultery. While the verse suggests sexual promiscuity, its reference is to Baal worship.[6] The Israelites have forsaken God and have gone after other gods. By doing so, they have breached the Sinai covenant and violated Torah.[7] A people no longer standing in right relationship with their divine partner in commitment, they evoke God's anger:

> Shall I not punish them for these things?…
> and shall I not bring retribution
> on a nation such as this? (v. 9)

What follows is an order given to the prophet by God (v. 10) and a further elucidation on Israel's transgressions and the people's self-assured, smug attitude (vv. 12–13).

Finally, verses 14–17 are a detailed description of how God plans to punish Israel because of its infidelity. Through the invasion and power of an enduring ancient nation, Israel will be decimated—its people, produce, plants, animals, and cities.[8]

In summary, Jeremiah 5:1–17 is a window into one aspect of Israel's life, while providing another glance at the community's theological beliefs. The text makes a clear ethical statement: A breach in a covenant relationship and a violation of Torah will incur serious repercussions that affect not only the social world but the natural world as well. Hence, human transgression and breach of right relationship cause all dimensions of creation to suffer, be they animals, plants, or cities (see v. 17).

From a theological perspective, the ethical message of the prophet is couched in and conditioned by the deuteronomistic theology of retribution. The message foreshadows a series of treacherous events that the Israelites can anticipate because of their choices, but none of these events should be surprising. According to Torah, failure to diligently observe God's commandments leads to being cursed by God in myriad ways (Deut. 28:15–68).

---

[6]For further discussion of the metaphorical language of verses 7–8, see ibid., 180–81.

[7]See, e.g., the Deuteronomic Code (Deut. 12:1–12) and the Decalogue (Ex. 20:2–7).

[8]The identity of the invading country and its warriors cannot be determined from the text. Additionally, it is not possible to know whether this event was a sudden invasion or an extended occupation. For further discussion, see Walter Brueggemann, *A Commentary on Jeremiah: Exile and Homecoming* (Grand Rapids, Mich.: Eerdmans, 1998), 65–66.

From a contemporary perspective, Jeremiah 5:1–17 raises a whole host of ideas with respect to how readers hear the ethical message of this prophet today. Through Jeremiah, one encounters a God who plans to deal with transgression with an assertion of power that has as its end destruction, not reconciliation. God will punish Israel by using another nation to wreak havoc on Israel's world. Justice will be accomplished through violence. Is this an ethical solution?

Finally, verses 4–5b contain material that calls for further consideration, especially when Jeremiah 5:1–17 is heard in a variety of contemporary contexts and from different perspectives. These verses portray the prophet making a comment about two groups of people, the poor and the rich:

> Then I said, "These are only the poor,
> they have no sense;
> for they do not know the way of the LORD,
> the law of their God.
> Let me go to the rich
> and speak to them;
> surely they know the way of the LORD,
> the law of their God.

To whom these two groups of people refer is not certain from the text. Nor is it clear what type of poverty or wealth is being implied.[9] Regardless of what type of poverty is being implied, the poor do not seem to be as highly regarded by the prophet as the rich. From the perspective of someone who does not have economic, political, social, or intellectual status, this verse could be heard negatively, since it suggests that only one particular class of people has sense and the capacity to know the ways and law of God. The irony in the verse is that those who are expected to be more sensible than the poor, specifically the rich, are not (v. 5c). Thus, while presenting a view of the entire Israelite community as corrupt, the text does reflect a certain prejudgment of the poor on the part of the prophet, who, according to the text, seems to presume otherwise about the rich. Heard in a contemporary setting, the point of classism

---

[9] There is nothing in the text that would allow for specific identification of either the poor or the rich. With respect to the poor, Holladay suggests that "sometimes they are simply the opposite of the rich (Ruth 3:10), but not always; sometimes they are simply the powerless and insignificant, as opposed to those with power and influence (Lev. 19:15), and so here. In the city streets and squares (v. 1) they would be the petty merchants and peddlers, craftsmen and porters crowding and shouting" (*Jeremiah 1*, 178). J. A. Thompson suggests that the poor may be a reference to those who have a "poverty of knowledge and understanding rather than poverty of an economic kind" (*The Book of Jeremiah* [Grand Rapids, Mich.: Eerdmans, 1980], 237–38). The rich could refer to those with economic wealth or those with power (e.g., the kings, priests, and prophets) or both.

comes to the fore, which begs the questions: For someone who is as concerned about justice and righteousness as the prophet is, how ethical are the prophet's assumptions? and, To what extent do such assumptions continue to influence how some people might view and/or stereotype others?

In sum, Jeremiah 5:1–17 comments on the social and religious situation that has ethical implications for that community. At the same time, the text evokes new ideas and questions for further ethical reflection.

Ezekiel 6:1–7

Israel stands accused of not only apostasy but also idolatry. In Ezekiel 6:1–7 the prophet receives a divine word (v. 1) that instructs him to set his face toward the mountains of Israel and preach against them (v. 2) a word of their impending doom because of their idolatry (vv. 3–7). The prophecy of judgment begins in verse 3. The prophet announces that God is going to wield a sword that will destroy apostate members of the Israelite community as well as their high places (v. 3).[10] The altars of idolatrous worship will be made desolate, and the incense stands will be broken (v. 4). Additionally, God will throw the slain in front of the community's idols and scatter the bones of the dead around the altars (v. 5), thereby denying them a burial for a proper final rest.[11] Furthermore, the towns where the people live, as well as other artifacts, will also be destroyed (v. 6). Those who survive the sword will know that God is the Lord (v. 7). They will have seen the powerlessness of the idols when confronted by God's power, and they will have experienced the futility of idol worship when no intervention on their behalf comes in the face of God's wrath.

This passage brings to the fore the practice of idolatry that existed within the Israelite community, a practice that breached covenant relationship and violated Torah.[12] The passage also describes an intended course of action whereby divine power would be used violently and destructively as a sign of judgment against idolatry and idol worship. Clearly,

---

[10]The reference to "mountains of Israel" in verse 2 along with the mention of the "mountains" and the "hills" and the "ravines and the valleys" in verse 3 figuratively symbolize the whole land of Israel, as well as the Israelite community, particularly its leadership and the community's idolatrous places of worship. For further discussion, see Daniel I. Block, *The Book of Ezekiel: Chapters 1—24*, NICOT (Grand Rapids, Mich.: Eerdmans, 1997), 221–23; and Lamar Eugene Cooper, Sr., *Ezekiel*, NAC, vol. 17 (Nashville: Broadman & Holman, 1994), 107.

[11]Block notes that "the exposure of the corpses on the hilltops represents an open invitation to vultures and other scavenging creatures, and is symptomatic of the bone that hangs over the sinful population (*Ezekiel*, 228). Thus, the scattering of the corpses' bones around the altars vivifies not only how treacherous idolatry was considered to be but also how much of an abomination it was to God.

[12]See, e.g., Exodus 19:5–6 and 20:2–6; cf. Deuteronomy 12:29–32.

the prophet's message and the description of God's plan of action reflect various cultural and religious influences of the ancient world that, for contemporary readers and listeners of Ezekiel 6:1–7, could raise a variety of theological and ethical questions about the use and abuse of power.

In summary, Ezekiel 6:1–7 exposes the idolatrous practices of some members within the ancient Israelite community that result in a stinging message of judgment from the prophet, which in turn invites ongoing ethical and theological reflection.

Hosea 8:1–14

Hosea 8:1–14 continues the theme of Israel's idolatry.The passage is a vivid example of Israel's breach of covenant relationship and blatant disregard for Torah and is composed of three units: verses 1–3, a cry of warning, verses 4–13, a description of Israel's political and cultic transgressions, and verse 14, a statement of divine judgment. Similar to Isaiah 1:2–9, Jeremiah 5:1–17, and Ezekiel 6:1–7, the Hosea passage elicits further ethical and theological reflection with respect to the statement of divine judgment in verse 14.

Verses 1–3, the first unit, set the stage for the sequence of events that follow, all of which lead up to the statement of divine judgment in verse 14.Verse 1a opens with a strong imperative spoken by God through the prophet and addressed to an individual: "Set the trumpet to your lips!" The remainder of the verse states the reason for the alarm, "One like a vulture is over the house of the LORD" (v. 1a, b), and why the people are in danger, "because they have broken my covenant, and transgressed my law" (v. 1b). Here, "law" refers to Torah as "instruction," as will be seen in verses 4–13. Members of the Israelite community have not followed the teachings and ways of God. In verse 2, God quotes the community. The statement is ironic because in verse 3, God accuses Israel of spurning the good. Because of this, the enemy—the "vulture" (v. 1)—will pursue Israel; ironically, this enemy, this vulture, is already over the house of Israel.[13]

Verses 4–13 outline the issues and transgressions violating covenant and law that lead the Israelites away from Torah and away from God. First, Israel set up kings independent of God and princes without God's

---

[13]The "vulture" and "enemy" to which verses 1–3 refer is probably Assyria. Bruce Birch argues that "this speech comes from the time just before or after 733 BC when Assyria was threatening and actually annexed much of Israel's northern territory" (*Hosea, Joel, and Amos*, West BC [Louisville, Ky.: Westminster John Knox Press, 1997], 78). Douglas Stuart concurs and points out that "Israel's ultimate enemy is Yahweh" (*Hosea-Jonah*, WordBC 31 [Waco, Tex.: Word Books, 1987]). From Israel's perspective and understanding of God and God's ways, this would be accurate, since the Assyrian invasion would be interpreted by the Israelite community as an act sanctioned, if not caused, by God. See Deuteronomy 28:49.

knowledge.[14] This is problematic because the community had been instructed by God through Moses that the people could indeed set up a king, but the person had to be one chosen by God (Deut. 17:14–15).[15] Hence, political leadership was established without divine initiation, consultation, or approval. Such acts violate covenant.

The indictment against Israel for its idolatry comes in verse 4b:"With their silver and gold they made idols for their own destruction." Idolatry violates the law (see Ex. 20:3f.; 34:17; Lev. 19:4) and goes against the sense of covenant of which the law is a part. Both covenant and law forbade the construction and worship of idols (see Deut. 4:23 and Hos. 8:1b).

Verses 5–6, with their reference to the calf of Samaria, recall Exodus 32:1–35, which tells of the Israelites' making a golden calf from their jewelry while Moses was on Mount Sinai. The verses are addressed to the people of Samaria, the capital city of the Northern Kingdom, Israel. The "calf of Samaria" (v. 6) is to be understood as the bull that Jeroboam I had erected in Bethel (1 Kings 12:29).[16] The bull is the symbol for the Canaanite god Baal. Just as the people have spurned the good, namely, God and God's ways, so God will reject the people's calf and break it to pieces. Thus, the Israelites live under the shadow of God's judgment, a theme that continues in the next three verses of the passage.

Verses 7–10 describe Israel's political situation. The country is powerless:

Israel is swallowed up;
now they are among the nations
as a useless vessel. (v. 8)

Israel offered tribute to Assyria before the Assyrian invasion and conquest made it obligatory (vv. 8–9). Wolff notes that "Israel is a precious, desirable, notable people among the nations only as her God's free covenant people."[17] Furthermore, Ephraim—the Northern Kingdom Israel—"has bargained for lovers" (v. 9). Wolff notes further that

the whore Ephraim who surrenders herself is not even worth enough to her political "lovers" to receive a harlot's wages from them. She has to pay them! With this, Hosea transfers his metaphor

---

[14]Stuart points out that the historical backdrop to verse 4a is the "rapid-fire succession of Northern kings, most assuming power by assassination (2 Kings 15:8–30)" that occurred sometime after 748 B.C.E. (*Hosea-Jonah*, 131). He adds further that "it was the way that kings were imposed and deposed that God rejected"(132).

[15]See also 1 Samuel 16:1–13; 2 Samuel 5:3; 1 Kings 1:11, 18; 19:15–16.

[16]Hans Walter Wolff suggests that "the calf of Samaria" should also be understood as "another expression for 'royal sanctuary' and 'temple of the kingdom' designating the temple of Bethel (Am 7:13)." See Wolff, *Hosea*, trans. Gary Stansell, Hermeneia (Philadelphia: Fortress Press, 1974), 140.

[17]Wolff, *Hosea*, 142.

of the prostitute from the cultic sphere to that of Israel's foreign policy.[18]

Despite Israel's negotiations with other countries, it will have to endure God's judgment: God will gather the people up, and they will suffer under the burden of corrupt kings and princes not of their own country. The verses foreshadow Israel's deportation to Assyria, which, for the Israelite people, could be interpreted as God's curse and judgment for the breach of covenant and the violation of Torah (see Deut. 28:36–37).

Verses 11–13 shed light on Israel's religious practices and cultic sins. Verse 12, a pivotal verse, features the unit's main point: Israel has disregarded Torah—God's instructions are looked upon as "a strange thing." Thus, the multiple altars for the expiation of sins become altars of sinning (v. 11), and the sacrifices offered to God are consequently rejected by God (v. 13a). In verse 13b, divine judgment is cast upon Israel: God will remember the people's iniquity and punish their sins; they will return to Egypt, to the place where they had once experienced bondage.

The passage closes on a somber note:

> Israel has forgotten his Maker,
> and built palaces;
> and Judah has multiplied fortified cities;
> but I will send a fire upon his cities,
> and it shall devour his strongholds. (v. 14)

Amnesia is the root of all Israel's problems. Israel has forgotten its God and has taken refuge in political and military strength by means of building palaces and multiplying fortified cities. The false security will, however, end in folly at the moment of divine judgment, when fire will consume the strongholds.

In summary, Hosea 8:1–14 provides a vivid picture of Israel and its struggles. The nation is (1) guilty of idolatry, (2) considered useless by other nations, (3) disloyal, (4) hypocritical, (5) forgetful, and (6) living under divine judgment. Israel has broken covenant and transgressed the law. For readers then and now, the prophet delivers a powerful message, and yet, one questions the ethical aspect of the prophet's word, which promises destruction in the face of infidelity.

Micah 1:2–7

Perhaps one of the most ringing invectives aimed at the Israelite community on account of its idolatry and apostate ways is found in the

---

[18]Ibid., 143.

book of Micah, specifically in Micah 1:2–7. This unit, a judgment speech, features the prophet Micah issuing a universal call to attention to human beings and the natural world (v. 2).[19] Both are the recipients of the prophet's foreboding message (vv. 3–7), one that includes an underlying sentiment of divine disdain at the people's infidelity, which will result in severe chastisement by God (vv. 6–7).

A theophany follows the prophet's call to attention (vv. 3–4). Here Micah announces that indeed the Lord is leaving the divine abode to come down and tread upon the high places of the earth (v. 3).[20] Such an event anticipates a response from the natural world: The mountains will melt like wax near the fire, and the valleys will burst open like waters poured down a steep place (v. 4). The scene is one of complete disintegration that highlights the power of God and the powerlessness of creation.

Verse 5 describes the cause for such turmoil. With a simple statement and a series of rhetorical questions, Micah indicts the people of Israel and Judah, who are guilty of sin and transgression. Verses 6–7 depict a wrathful God, incensed over the people's actions. Speaking through Micah, this God announces a grave plan that is to befall the city of Samaria, leaving it and its idols in ruins. Here, Samaria represents Jacob/Israel, the Northern Kingdom, whose fate foreshadows what is to be the lot of of the Southern Kingdom Judah as well (see v. 5c in context with vv. 8–14).

It is clear from verses 6–7 that the people of Israel have broken covenant with their God; they stand condemned and guilty of idol worship and apostasy. Gender-specific images crystallize Micah's message: Female Samaria will become a heap, a place for planting vineyards. God will pour down "her" stones into the valley and uncover "her" foundations (v. 6). All "her" images shall be beaten to pieces, "her" wages burned with fire, and "her" idols laid waste because "she" has played the harlot:

for as the wages of a prostitute she gathered them,
and as the wages of a prostitute they shall again be used. (v. 7)

---

[19] Wolff argues against such a cosmological reading and asserts that the verse refers to "human beings who are capable of listening (as in Isa. 23:1)." See Wolff, *Micah,* trans. Gary Stansell, Continental Commentary (Minneapolis: Augsburg Fortress Press, 1990), 54. Wolff's argument suggests an anthropocentric reading and hearing of the text.

[20] The phrase "high places of the earth" is obscure. One suggestion is that it refers to the mountains, or it could refer to handmade constructions often built on elevated places (see Jer. 48:35 and Isa. 15:2). "High places" are also associated with idolatry (2 Kings 23:5–8) and as such become the objects of God's wrath (Lev. 26:30; 2 Kings 17:5–23; and Ps. 78:58). In light of Micah 1:5, the "high places" could also refer to the capital cities of Samaria and Jerusalem, two political and religious centers that represent the nations' infidelity and transgressions. For further comment on "the high places" in Micah 1:3–5, see Carol J. Dempsey, "The Interplay between Literary Form and Technique and Ethics in Micah 1—3" (Ph.D. diss. The Catholic University of America, 1994), 96–100.

Thus, female Samaria, representing all of Israel, and female Jerusalem, representing all of Judah (see v. 5), are unfaithful to God, who is viewed as a male figure (v. 3).[21]

Viewing verses 2–7 as a whole, readers see that Israel and Judah have acted unethically; here, Israel is specified. The people have violated Torah, have disregarded covenant, and have fallen out of right relationship with God, a situation that will have serious consequences. Readers also hear the voice of a prophet announcing the coming of a powerful God who promises to mete out justice through destruction.

Furthermore, readers also hear a prophetic message of judgment couched in feminine images. The people's unethical behavior warranted an ethical response from the prophet, but the Micah passage raises additional ethical questions for readers, questions that need further reflection. To what extent does the use of gender-specific metaphors to describe a country's ills lead to patriarchal assumptions and oppressive practices on the part of those who have received the biblical text? To what degree does Micah's message confirm within one's theological and social imagination the practice of distributing power hierarchically and patriarchally? Finally, the vision of God that the prophet proclaims is a God who will come and punish the people violently because of their infidelity. This God is a God of power who uses power punitively and thus sends a strong message to readers: Be faithful or else! Given the fact that the biblical text as a whole is theologically, historically, and culturally conditioned, readers are confronted with a further question: How does one appropriate the use of power when used violently and punitively to resolve conflict, and to what degree does the prophet's God reflect the picture of the human condition of his day?[22]

Apostasy and Idolatry in Context

Selected texts from the books of Isaiah, Jeremiah, Ezekiel, Hosea, and Micah indicate that within the ancient Israelite community, apostasy and idolatry existed. This situation provoked a response from several of the community's religious leaders, namely the prophets, who exposed the people's transgressions and warned them of the serious implications their actions would have on their future life and their relationship with God. The prophets' messages also make known to the people that their transgressions will have an adverse effect on creation as well. Hence, loss

---

[21]Note the male possessive pronouns associated with God in verse 5. Cities are often designated as feminine nouns in the Hebrew language and Hebrew biblical text.

[22]For additional comment on Micah 1:2–7, see Carol J. Dempsey, *The Prophets: A Liberation-Critical Reading* (Minneapolis: Fortress Press, 2000), 24–26. Several points made in this study allude to material and ideas developed further in the Dempsey volume.

of right relationship with God affects all other relationships. From a contemporary cosmological and eco-ethical perspective, the prophets' proclamations hint at the link that exists between human transgression and the suffering of the natural world, a link in need of a prophetic response from hearers and readers of the biblical passages today.

Additionally, readers see from this series of selected texts on apostasy and idolatry that Israel's God, who entered into covenant with the Israelites, and who entrusted them with Torah, will not tolerate being forgotten and forsaken. Isaiah, Jeremiah, Ezekiel, Hosea, and Micah make clear to the people of their day that God will dole out to the apostate and idolatrous ones their "just deserts." This ethical message that the prophets deliver to their people suggests to contemporary readers a variety of questions in need of ongoing theological and ethical reflection if the prophetic word is to be understood first in its original historical, social, and cultural contexts and then reinterpreted for believing communities today.

Political and Religious Corruption

Ancient Israel struggled not only with apostasy and idolatry but also with social injustice that stemmed in part from the lack of ethical conduct and decisions on the part of the people's political and religious leaders. These leaders in many cases failed to embrace Torah as a way of life and therefore neglected their ethical responsibility to act with justice and righteousness on behalf of the community's members and to call them to do likewise, with the understanding that if community members failed to do so, they would be held accountable for their unethical behavior. Examples of corrupt leadership are mentioned in several texts of Isaiah, Jeremiah, Hosea, Micah, Zephaniah, and Zechariah, who denounce the political and religious leaders of their day and expose their unethical ways that cause others to suffer unjustly.

Isaiah 10:1–4

In this woe proclamation, the prophet Isaiah takes to task the political leaders of his day who are depriving the most vulnerable, specifically the needy, the poor, the widows, and the orphans, of their rights. Such deprivation allows those in power to oppress others for the purposes of self-interest and gain.[23] Isaiah rails against such leaders directly and uninhibitedly:

---

[23]To whom this woe proclamation is addressed is not clear, given the scholarly debate over its placement in Isaiah 1—39. For further discussion on both these points see Dempsey, *The Prophets*; Walter Brueggemann, *Isaiah 1—39*, WestBC (Louisville, Ky.: Westminster John Knox Press, 1998), 86–91; and Otto Kaiser, *Isaiah 1—12*, OTL (Philadelphia: Westminster Press, 1972), 63–71.

Ah, you who make iniquitous decrees,
who write oppressive statutes,
to turn aside the needy from justice
and to rob the poor of my people of their right,
that widows may be your spoil,
and that you may make the orphans your prey! (vv. 1–2)

Whether the "iniquitous decrees" refer to unjust decisions based on existing laws or to the devising and enforcing of new laws that caused oppression to some and not to others is a matter of scholarly debate, but it seems likely that both situations could have occurred in Isaiah's time.[24]

Whether such decrees were old or new is irrelevant to the issue at hand: The leaders of Isaiah's day were perpetrators of injustice. Oswalt notes clearly the ethical problem:

> It is one thing when competition or rank and favor pits person against person and region against region. It is another when persons begin consciously to deprive the helpless of their rights in order to oppress them. At this point, the lowest limits of cynicism and self-serving have been reached. The brutal nature of warfare and conquest can at least be mashed with the trappings of destiny and courage. Oppression of the helpless has no such coverings. Its essential ugliness cannot be hidden. It was especially unjustified in a society where equal treatment before the law was understood to grow out of the very character of God (Exod. 23:6–9; Lev. 9:15; Deut. 10:17; 16:19; 24:17).[25]

After Isaiah exposes the corruption of the leaders of his day and indicts them directly and severely, he asks them two rhetorical questions (vv. 3–4). These questions foreshadow the divine judgment and chastisement that is to befall them because of their unethical behavior (v. 3a) and point up their powerlessness in the face of the forthcoming day of reckoning (vv. 3b–4a). The lot of the oppressed will, in turn, become the fate of the oppressors.

Isaiah concludes his address with a simple statement that conveys divine outrage over the sociopolitical situation that existed in his day:

For all this his anger has not turned away;
his hand is stretched out still. (v. 4b)

---

[24]For further discussion see John N. Oswalt, *The Book of Isaiah: Chapters 1—39*, NICOT (Grand Rapids, Mich.: Eerdmans, 1986), 259, which cites representative scholarly views on both interpretations of "iniquitous decrees," and which also suggests that these decrees could have been both new ones and already existing ones that were applied unjustly to certain people.

[25]Ibid. Two changes in Oswalt's quote have been made for the purpose of inclusive language.

The divine hand that was once extended for the purpose of Israel's salvation and liberation from Egyptian oppression (see, e.g., Ex. 13:3; 15:6) is now extended in judgment against certain oppressive members of the Israelite community whose ancestors were a people once oppressed themselves. For contemporary readers of this text, the face of the God of justice shines brightly in the face of human injustice, but a further question surfaces in relation to Isaiah 10:1–4: What kind of God is Isaiah's God, whose anger at such injustice moves this Divine One to seek justice for the oppressed in a way that would seem to be punitive and deadly rather than constructive (see, e.g., 10:5–6; compare 5:8–30)?

Isaiah 28:1–29

Isaiah continues his indictment against the leaders of his day in Isaiah 28:1–29. Added to his list of corrupt political leaders are those religious leaders—priests and prophets—who have succumbed to self-indulgence at the expense of their religious duties (vv. 7–13). This passage consists of five units: a woe proclamation (vv. 1–4); a vision of hope (vv. 5–6); an indictment against specific religious leaders (vv. 7–13); a judgment speech (vv. 14–22); and a parable (vv. 23–29).

In verses 1–4, Isaiah addresses the Northern Kingdom Israel. He accuses the people of inordinate self-indulgence (v. 1)[26] and warns them of impending action by God (v. 2), action that will result in their devastation (vv. 3–4). Images of the proud garland of the drunkards of Ephraim and the fading flower on the head of those bloated with rich food is recapitulated and expanded on in verses 3–4 to add a sense of unity to the prophet's woe and to intensify his harrowing message. The entire unit foreshadows the Assyrian invasion of the Northern Kingdom, to be led by Tiglath-pileser III, the "one" who is "mighty and strong," who will hurl down to the earth these drunkards and gluttons "like a storm of hail," a "destroying tempest," "a storm of mighty, overflowing waters" (v. 2).

Both the prophet's message and the text suggest to readers that God is an all-powerful and controlling God who is capable of creating weal and woe to serve as a corrective for irresponsible behavior, and who will use other people, in this case another nation, to accomplish the divine task and teach a painful lesson. Viewing the unit from a historical perspective and in its historical context, Walter Brueggemann comments:

The poem asserts not only the inevitability of Assyria (cf 10:5–19), but also the large, magisterial governance of Yahweh over

---

[26]This life of self-indulgence could be literal or metaphorical. See Brueggemann, who comments that "the reference may be literal [that is, irresponsible alcohol], or it may be metaphorical [referring to a life of narcoticized indifference] (*Isaiah 1—39*, 221).

the entire international process. Imperial expansionism does not just happen. It reflects the moral agenda of Yahweh, who dispatches the rise and fall of nations.[27]

Although this unit reflects the theological beliefs and historical situation of Isaiah's day, and perhaps the attitudes and beliefs of the prophet himself and the text's later editors and redactors, such a text inspires ongoing theological reflection and critique, particularly with respect to the image of God proclaimed by the prophet and God's "moral agenda" and participation in geopolitical affairs as highlighted by Brueggemann.

The prophet's foreboding message of judgment with its dismal tone shifts in verses 5–6. Here, Isaiah delivers a message of hope to his listeners. A new day will dawn, one of promise, not devastation. Debauchery and defeat will give way to renewal and restoration, but only for the "remnant" of the people, not to Israel as a whole (v. 5). God will empower the one who sits in judgment with a spirit of justice; to those who turn back the battle at the gate, God will give strength (v. 6). The text suggests that among the remnant will be just and strong judicial and military leadership that will arise from the country's ash heaps and ruins (vv. 1–4).

In verses 7–13, Isaiah indicts the religious leaders of his day—the priest and the prophet—who, because of their overindulgence in strong drink (vv. 7a, b, 8) have compromised their religious offices and duties: "They err in vision, they stumble in giving judgment"(v. 7c). In verses 9–10, Isaiah quotes the response that the religious leaders offer as a retort to the prophet's indictment of them. Verses 11–13 are Isaiah's response to the retort in 9–10. Indeed the prophet—the one who has not compromised the prophetic office and religious responsibilities—will speak to those who have (vv. 11–12), and the word spoken will not be a compassionate one. They will be made to suffer the consequences of their actions (v. 13).

In verses 14–22, Isaiah addresses the rulers of Judah, specifically those of Jerusalem (v. 14). He first quotes them, exposing their illicit deeds (v. 15),[28] and then casts judgment on them (vv. 17–22);[29] but to those

---

[27]Ibid.

[28]The identity of those "who rule this people in Jerusalem" is unclear from the text. It may refer to Jerusalem's rulers in general, as suggested by Oswalt (*The Book of Isaiah: Chapters 1—39*, 516), or it could refer to the priests and prophets in verse 7 as Brueggemann suggests (*Isaiah 1—39*, 225). For additional comment, see Christopher R. Seitz, *Isaiah 1—39*, Interpretation (Louisville, Ky.: John Knox Press, 1993), 209–10. Clearly, Isaiah's indictment is against the country's leaders, be they political, cultic, or both.

[29]There are multiple suggestions for verse 15. The verse could refer to a political alliance made with Egypt or some sort of pact made with the gods of the underworld. See Seitz, *Isaiah 1—39*, 209–10; and Oswalt, *The Book of Isaiah: Chapters 1—39*, 516–17. What is clear is that Jerusalem's leaders have become involved in some sort of unethical action that the prophet Isaiah does not allow to go unnoticed or unheard.

who hold steadfast to God and God's ways, there is a message of hope and comfort (v. 16). In verses 17–21 the prophet makes known God's thoughts: God will not tolerate such despicable behavior on the part of Jerusalem's leaders. God will rise up against them with power and might, rendering them and their covenant powerless. Isaiah's final word to the rulers sums up his message to them (v. 14) and assures them that God's action against them will affect the whole land as well (v. 22).

Verses 23–29, the last unit of Isaiah 28:1–29, feature Isaiah trying to teach his listeners a lesson about God and God's ways. The rich agricultural and pastoral images embedded in this unit suggest to Isaiah's listeners and later readers of the text that indeed God's final word is not a word of destruction; it is a word of hope. How farmers clear and cultivate their land is an instruction that seems to sum up God's intended actions in verses 17–22 while adding a twist to them. The threatened leveling of Jerusalem/Judah, with the inclusion of its corrupted leaders implied (v. 22), has as its purpose not everlasting destruction but rather a threshing for the sake of replanting (compare Jer. 1:10). God will restore the land and the people, and will restore the land and the people to each other and to God, but not without first overturning the land and its inhabitants.

In summary, Isaiah 28:1–29 features the prophet Isaiah taking to task the leaders of his day, namely those priests and prophets who have become self-indulgent to the point of neglecting the duties of their respective offices. The text makes clear that the role of prophet is to expose the unethical ways of others, leaders in particular, and to communicate to people down through the ages that such conduct is not divinely ordained or sanctioned. The text, however, also calls readers to reconsider the prophet's depiction of God, who metes out justice to one group of people by means of another more powerful group, who will accomplish the divine task in a destructive rather than constructive way. Hence, the ethical message of Isaiah invites further ethical reflection.

Jeremiah 2:26–28

Like Isaiah, Jeremiah also attacks the leaders of his day. Addressing the house of Israel (v. 26) and Judah (v. 28), Jeremiah delivers God's indictment against not only the people but also their kings, their officials, their priests, and their prophets (v. 26), all of whom have turned their backs to God, preferring to worship idols (v. 27). These apostate people have violated covenant and Torah and are forewarned that in their time of trouble, their gods will not be able to save them (v. 28). All have transgressed against God, and worst of all, the rulers of the people, who were the keepers and instructors of Torah, were no better than the people whom they served.

The religious decay of both kingdoms is apparent and does not go unnoticed or unaddressed by the prophet, who communicates God's word of disdain. By doing so, Jeremiah calls his listeners and readers to faithfulness and highlights the ethical responsibility that is part of a leader's office and task: to remain in right relationship with God and to uphold Torah as an attitude and way of life that safeguards covenant.

Jeremiah 5:12–17

The religious leaders of Jeremiah's day continue to be the subject of derision in Jeremiah 5:12–17.[30] In this passage, Jeremiah indicts those prophets who have delivered false prophecies. The unit opens with God's speaking through Jeremiah, making a case against those who have corrupted their prophetic office.[31] God first makes a judgment statement against them (v. 12a), then bolsters the argument by quoting what they have said (v. 12b, c), and concludes with a brief summation:

> The prophets are nothing but wind,
> for the word is not in them.
> Thus shall it be done to them! (v. 13)

The summation leads into verses 14–17, a divine judgment speech. Here, Jeremiah proclaims God's ringing message, which God addresses not only to Jeremiah but also to the entire house of Israel that will be made to suffer on account of those prophets who have spoken falsely to the people, failing to call them to repent of their transgressions (5:1–11). In essence, the prophets who have spoken falsely have shirked the responsibility of their office, and in doing so, have led the people astray, allowing them to wallow in their sinfulness and waywardness (see Jer. 5:6–9). Therefore, God will make Jeremiah's words fire and the people wood that will be consumed by the flame (v. 14). Through an enemy nation, enduring and ancient, God plans to devastate the house of Israel— its people, livestock, land, and cities (vv. 15–17). Israel's God, who some prophets said will do nothing (v. 12a), pledges to act with vengeance. And the house of Israel that was once assured of security (v. 12b) is now forewarned of extraordinary devastation (vv. 14b–17).

---

[30]Two other notable passages in which Jeremiah takes religious leaders to task are Jeremiah 5:30–31 and 23:9–15.

[31]William L. Holladay argues that the speaker of verses 12–13 is Yahweh (*Jeremiah 1*, 185). Contrary to Holladay, I suggest that these verses are a Yahweh speech that continues verses 10–11 and leads into verses 12–17, another speech by Yahweh. The reference to Yahweh/ "the Lord" (in English) in the third person in Yahweh speeches is not atypical. See, e.g., Isaiah 49:7; Micah 2:12–13; 4:6–7.

This passage portrays Jeremiah standing in sharp contrast to those prophets of his day who are prophesying falsely. Ronald E. Clements points out that

> Jeremiah stands as a starkly religious and moral prophet…He accuses the people of moral obtuseness and allows no room for a heroic patriotism. Nor does Jeremiah give room to support what must have been the popular belief: God would intervene directly to save Israel since it was a divinely elect nation. The prophetic message from Jeremiah is unremittingly personal and inward-looking in its uncovering of the personal and individual nature of sin.[32]

Jeremiah, the one consecrated by God before birth to be a prophet, remains steadfast in his vocation and faithful to the responsibility of his office: He delivers God's word, as harsh as it is, to prophets and people alike.

In summary, Jeremiah 5:12–17 suggests to readers a portrait of a prophet who is able to maintain his personal integrity in the midst of communal depravity. Bearing witness to God's word, he reveals to his hearers and readers a God who will not remain silent or inactive in the face of religious infidelity and transgression (see vv. 11, 12–17). This image of God that the prophet and text portray, however, is troublesome. Readers see Jeremiah delivering, unquestioningly, a message that depicts a God of punitive justice whose mission is accomplished through another in a way that is violent and devastating to both human and nonhuman life.[33]

Hosea 4:4–11

Hosea also knows complacent religious leaders. Following his enumeration of Israel's transgressions (vv. 1–3), Hosea indicts the priests of his day while mentioning the prophets, who have neglected their responsibilities to the detriment of the Israelite community. Part of a longer accusation (vv. 1–11), verses 4–11 describe God's contention with the priests: They have rejected knowledge and have forgotten the law of their God. Consequently, the people are "destroyed for lack of knowledge" (v. 6). Furthermore, the priests are profiting personally from the people's transgressions, since they receive a certain portion of the atonement offerings that the guilty ones bring to the sanctuaries (v. 8).[34]

---

[32] Ronald E. Clements, *Jeremiah,* Interpretation (Atlanta: John Knox Press, 1988), 42.

[33] For further comment on this passage, see Dempsey, *The Prophets*, 41–44.

[34] On the relationship between guilt offerings and the profits of the priesthood, see Birch, *Hosea, Joel, and Amos*, 52.

God's response to the priests' infidelities and deplorable deeds is candid and without compassion. Hosea declares that God will destroy their mothers (v. 5); reject them as priests (v. 6); forget their children (v. 6);[35] punish them for their ways (v. 9); repay them for their deeds (v. 9); and allow them to experience no personal satisfaction from their gain or deeds (v. 10). Without a doubt, certain religious leaders—here, the priest—have corrupted their offices and neglected their responsibilities. For Hosea, the priests' behavior becomes an ethical issue, as Birch outlines:

> Hosea goes straight to the central charge against the priests of Israel. They have "rejected knowledge" (v. 6a), and "forgotten the law of God" (v. 6b)…[T]he knowledge of God for Hosea…is at the heart of covenant commitment. Here Hosea places such knowledge as parallel to "the law [torah] of God." The Hebrew word *torah* means "instruction" both as process and as content. It is the way in which God's covenant will be made known and incorporated into Israel's life. The result would be a people filled with the "knowledge of God." And the priest had the leadership responsibility to see that this happened. The priest was to instruct the people. The priest was to know and teach the Torah. The priest was the custodian and steward of the "knowledge of God" in the midst of Israel[36]

Corruption within the priesthood does not go unnoticed by Hosea and, according to the prophet, will not go unchecked by God.

To contemporary readers, Hosea 4:4–11 suggests that in ancient Israel there were problems within the cult that demanded an ethical response from those prophets who, like Hosea, spoke out because of their fidelity to God and the ensuing responsibilities that such a commitment brings. Hosea's ethical response, however, invites continued ethical and theological reflection, particularly with respect to the comment that the priest's mother would be destroyed and the children forgotten (see vv. 5 and 6). While such metaphorical language intensifies the prophet's message and may even strike the heart of the accused, it raises a problem: Should someone be made to suffer as a chastisement for another's transgression as the text suggests? Even if the language is metaphorical, it communicates an attitude

---

[35]Birch suggests that the reference to God's forgetting the children and similarly to destroying the priest's mother in verse 5b are not to be understood literally. The text infers that "the priest who has rejected knowledge will have no past or future in Israel" (ibid., 52). While this may be the intention of the verse, one cannot overlook the fact that Hosea's reference is to two of the most vulnerable groups of people on the social ladder of his day—women and children—who will be made to suffer on account of the sins of, presumably, certain males in Hosea's social circle.

[36]Ibid., 51.

that sanctions justice at the expense of the society's least powerful, the most vulnerable—women and children (see note 35).

Micah 3:1–12

With bold and biting words, with images that strike at the people's moral consciousness, the prophet Micah lampoons the political and religious leaders of Israel as well. This passage can be divided into four units: an address to Israel's political leadership (vv. 1–4); a prophecy against Israel's prophets (vv. 5–7); an interlude (v. 8); and a second address to Israel's leadership, political and religious (vv. 9–12). In verses 1–4, Micah condemns Israel's political leaders for their brutal treatment of the kingdom's people. A rhetorical question followed by contrasting images and an extended metaphor vivify the prophet's message and accentuate the leaders' illicit deeds (vv. 2–3). Verse 4 presents God's response. Micah declares to the corrupted leaders that God will be unresponsive and somewhat distant from them. In verses 5–7, Micah takes to task the corrupted prophets who have led the people astray with their false prophecies (v. 5). Their fate will be God's suppression of their prophetic gifts (vv. 6–7).

Following two attacks on Israel's leadership, Micah offers a comment about himself and how he views his mission:

> But as for me, I am filled with power,
> with the spirit of the LORD,
> and with justice and might,
> to declare to Jacob his transgression
> and to Israel his sin (v. 8).

Here, Micah confidently states his prophetic gifts and makes clear to his listeners that his duty is to expose the injustices and sins of others. His stance is an ethical one that makes clear to his audience how different he is from those prophets who have abused their prophetic office and compromised their prophetic powers.

Micah returns to his attack on leadership in verses 9–11 and then issues a judgment (v. 12). In verse 11, Micah points out that corruption is also a characteristic of Israel's priesthood. Hence, spiritual depravity is extensive. Because of unjust leaders,

> Jerusalem shall become a heap of ruins,
> and the mountain of the house a wooded height. (v. 12b)

Neither the leaders nor the holy city will escape divine retribution; justice will be served.

In Micah 3:1–12, readers are once again confronted by irresponsible and unethical leaders. And once again, such conduct is neither condoned nor ignored. Micah has declared to Jacob his transgression and to Israel his sin (v. 8). Both prophet and text offer readers a sense of hope. The injustices of a country's leaders will, in time, be brought to light, but not without human beings' exercising their power to act ethically in a spirit of justice that is willing to confront issues candidly and thus go against the malaise of the day.[37]

Zephaniah 3:3–5

The prophet Zephaniah also paints a graphic picture of Israel's leaders who have gone astray from God and God's ways. Following a comment on the city of Jerusalem (vv. 1–2), Zephaniah comments on the city's leaders: Its officials are roaring lions (v. 3a); its judges are evening wolves (v. 3b); its prophets are reckless and faithless persons (v. 4a); and its priests have profaned what is sacred and have done violence to the law (v. 4b). He also makes a point of stating that the unjust, presumably the leaders, know no shame (v. 5b, c). Against this backdrop, Zephaniah offers a word of hope: The Lord within Jerusalem is righteous, does no wrong, and renders judgment every morning faithfully (v. 5).

For contemporary readers, the voices of such Israelite prophets as Zephaniah continue to be a beacon of light to those who would live under or in the midst of corrupt leadership. For those leaders guilty of shameless injustices, however, such voices can be a source of contention and aggravation. The important point made by both prophet and text, though, is that God's justice will prevail.

Political and Religious Corruption in Context

Various texts from selected prophets indicate that throughout Israel's history, irresponsible and corrupt leaders were to blame, in part, for the perpetration of injustice and unethical practices. The texts examined also suggest, however, that in spite of what may seem to be the worst of times, hope continues to be part of the drama of life. That hope is apparent through the character of such persons as Isaiah, Jeremiah, Micah, Hosea, and Zephaniah, who continually remind and call people to covenant and Torah—to right relationships with God and with one another.

These prophets and texts also attest to a God who is acutely aware of injustice and offended by infidelity and will thus act accordingly. The prophets' descriptions of God and how God deals with injustice and

---

[37]For additional comment on Micah 3:1–12, see Dempsey, "Micah 1—3," 187–228, and *The Prophets*, 28–31.

infidelity suggest the need for ongoing theological and ethical reflection in faith communities today by those who espouse and affirm a just but compassionate and nonviolent God (see Hos. 11:9).

Finally, Isaiah 10:1–4 and 28:1–29; Jeremiah 2:26–28 and 5:12–17; Hosea 4:4–11; Micah 3:1–12; and Zephaniah 3:3–5 suggest to readers today that ultimately, power does not rest in leadership; it rests with God, who can empower ordinary human beings in extraordinary ways so that they can look iniquity in the face, name it, and begin to deal with it for the sake of hastening the divine vision of universal salvation for all creation.

Social Injustices

Because life in Israel was essentially hierarchical, the erosion of justice on the part of some of Israel's political and religious leaders seems to have taken its toll on the common good. The writings of the prophets indicate that social injustice was a problem among the Israelites themselves because some had forgotten and forsaken God and God's ways. With covenant broken and Torah abandoned, the sense of maintaining and remaining in right relationship with God and with one another was not always the motive behind various actions and decisions. Various prophetic texts suggest that some Israelites became the prey of others of their own kin who were more powerful—politically, economically, and socially. And it seems that such situations often went unchecked by some of Israel's political and religious leaders, but not by those prophets in Israel who remained faithful to their mission.

Isaiah 5:8–30

Within the prophetic corpus, many passages highlight the different kinds of social injustice and abuses that existed in ancient Israel. One example is Isaiah 5:8–30, a prophecy addressed to Jerusalem/Judah (see 5:3). This text consists of a series of six woe proclamations (vv. 8–10, 11–17, 18–19, 20, 21, 22–30). The first woe highlights the plight of those people who have lost home and field to powerful landowners whose prosperity and wealth have increased through the exploitation of those less powerful.

> [Woe to] you who join house to house,
> who add field to field,
> until there is room for no one but you,
> and you are left to live alone
> in the midst of the land! (v. 8)[38]

---

[38]NRSV has "Ah"; MT reads *hoy*, "woe." Here the Hebrew text is preferred over the English.

According to Torah, all land belonged to God (Ex. 19:5) and was a gift from God to the Israelites (Lev. 25:23–24). After the land was distributed among the families, it was to be kept within each family (Lev. 25; Num. 27:1–11; 36:1–12), and possession of the land was safeguarded by the Jubilee Year (Lev. 25:23–28; Ezek. 46:16–18). The people were not free to dispose of the land as they wished, nor were they allowed to take another family's or neighbor's land. Thus, in verses 8–10, those who have taken the property of others have violated Torah, are guilty of an injustice, and will experience serious repercussions because of their actions.[39]

The next four woes describe the social climate of Jerusalem/Judah. Certain members of the community are self-indulgent and self-absorbed to the point of insensitivity with regard to the ways and works of God (vv. 11–12); others are bound to sin to the extent that they scoff at God and mock the plan of the Holy One (vv. 18–19); and still others pervert right judgment (v. 20) and are wise and shrewd in their own estimation (v. 21). The first part of the sixth woe (v. 22a–b) brings to light the situation of grand self-indulgence and thus recalls the first woe (v. 11a). The second part of the woe (v. 23) focuses on those who act unethically within the judicial system:

who acquit the guilty for a bribe,
and deprive the innocent of their rights!

Verse 23 makes clear that because of corruption within the legal structure, innocent people are made to suffer and become victims not only of those who perpetrate injustice but also of the system itself. And yet, the prophet Isaiah makes known to his audience and readers alike that social injustice and inappropriate conduct and attitudes will have unpleasant consequences (vv. 9–10, 13–17, 24–30).

Jeremiah 5:20–29

In considering Jeremiah 5:20–29, William L. Holladay comments, "This passage is a sterling description of social injustice as Jrm saw it…"[40] Addressed specifically to the people of the Southern Kingdom, this prophecy presents a picture of Judah's religious and social disintegration, which eventually leads to the downfall of the kingdom. With stubborn and rebellious hearts, people have turned away from God and God's ways

---

[39]This verse attests to the latifundism that existed in the eighth century B.C.E., whereby wealthy landowners changed an egalitarian society of small landowners into a well-developed, stratified society at the expense of those who were less wealthy and therefore less powerful. Included in this shift was the exploitation of the poor.

[40]Holladay, *Jeremiah 1*, 199.

(vv. 23–24; see also v. 22). Brueggemann points out that "Israel's heart, the organ of covenant (cf. 4:4), has become alienated from God."[41] Thus, they have neglected to love God, walk in God's ways, and serve God with all their hearts as Torah asks and covenant requires (see Deut. 10:12–13).

Found among such an unfaithful group of people are scoundrels who have exploited others unjustly and have become rich through their exploitation (vv. 26–28). Thus, the domestic situation is "a war between the rich and the poor as the law is twisted to favor the rich."[42] Verse 28 singles out the "orphan" and the "needy," who represent two of Israel's most vulnerable groups of people. Hence, the reference to the "orphan" and the "needy"[43] shows again the problem of social injustice in Judah, a problem that the prophet Jeremiah highlights and one that will evoke a divine response (v. 29).

Jeremiah 9:4–11

The theme of social injustice continues in Jeremiah 9:4–6, an indictment. Here the focus is on the people's speech. Verse 4 opens with Jeremiah's issuing a divine warning to his listeners, cautioning them to beware of their neighbors and to put no trust in any of their kin, for their kin are "supplanters" and every neighbor like a "slanderer." In verses 5–6 he then delivers a divine indictment, which, in turn, makes explicit the injustices that people are doing to one another through unjust speech:

> They all deceive their neighbors,
> and no one speaks the truth;
> they have taught their tongues to speak lies;
> they commit iniquity and are too weary to repent.
> Oppression upon oppression, deceit upon deceit!
> They refuse to know me, says the LORD.

Truthful speech has changed to slander and deception, giving way to iniquity that results in oppression. They have turned on one another because they have fallen out of right relationship with their God, a situation that affects their common life with one another. And again, both text and prophet make clear that this type of conduct, which causes unnecessary and inordinate pain and suffering, is unacceptable and will be addressed (see vv. 7–11).

---

[41]See Brueggemann, *A Commentary on Jeremiah,* 68.
[42]Holladay, *Jeremiah 1,* 198.
[43]Cf. Isaiah 1:16–17.

Amos 8:4–8

One of the more vivid passages that describe social injustice within the Israelite community is Amos 8:4–8. In this passage, Amos—direct and unrestrained—addresses a group of Israelites who have acted unethically on several counts. First, they have economically exploited the poor (v. 5). Torah insists that the Israelites care for the poor and the most vulnerable in the society.[44] Second, the poor are "made into bartered goods in human trade traffic."[45] And third, those doing the exploiting also are selling the sweepings of wheat from their harvests. This is another injustice done to the poor and a violation of Torah, which insists that the gleanings of the harvest be left for the poor (Lev. 19:9–10; 23:22).[46]

Finally, one can ascertain from the text and Amos' proclamation that the feast of the new moon and the Sabbath were impediments to those doing the exploiting because it curtailed their sales efforts:

> "When will the new moon be over
> so that we may sell grain;
> and the sabbath,
> so that we may offer wheat for sale?" (v. 5)

The last part of this passage indicates that justice on behalf of the poor will eventually be served. Verses 7–8 feature God's taking an oath, swearing never to forget any of the unethical deeds (v. 7), and promising to chastise the mercenaries and barterers (v. 8; see also vv. 9–14).

Micah 2:1–5, 8–9

In Micah 2:1–5 and 8–9, social injustice also emerges in the prophet's preaching as a topic of concern. Verses 1–4 are a classic woe proclamation aimed at those Israelites who, like those in Amos 8:4–8, are using their power to take advantage of others. In verses 1–2, Micah lists the social injustices done to others by those more powerful in the community who devise wicked and evil deeds and then do them. These deeds include coveting and seizing other's fields and houses, which, according to Torah, are forbidden (Ex. 20:17 *twice*; 34:24; Deut. 5:21). Certain people are also guilty of extortion: They cheat the homeowner and his house, and a people and their inheritance. Here, "inheritance" refers specifically to the land that belongs to God, which God gave to Israel as a gift with the command

---

[44]See, e.g., Deuteronomy 10:18; 14:29; 16:11, 14; 24:19, 20, 21; 26:12, 13; 27:19.
[45]See Dempsey, *The Prophets*, 20.
[46]See also Deuteronomy 24:21 and the book of Ruth, specifically 2:2, 7, 8, 15, 16, 19.

to respect it.[47] According to Torah, anyone who "oppresses" a neighbor is to make restitution and seek divine pardon (Lev. 6:1–7).

In verses 8–9 the list of injustices continues. In verse 8, those accused of devising and carrying out wicked and evil deeds in verses 1–2 now rise up "as an enemy" against God's people and strip the robe from the peaceful (v. 8). This act of taking another's cloak is a grievous offense. Israelite social law states that if a cloak is borrowed from a neighbor, it must be returned to that person before sunset so that the individual will have it as a covering during the night (see Ex. 22:26–27). Thus, the guilty parties have violated their own social law and disobeyed God's command (Ex. 20:17).

In verse 9, those who have risen up "as an enemy" are indicted for two more counts of injustice: They drive the Israelite women out of their pleasant houses, and they take away God's glory from the children forever. "Glory" refers to the land.[48] Thus, those among the most vulnerable in Israel's society—the women and the children—are prey to those who are more powerful. Together, verses 1–2 and verses 8–9 expose the corruption that existed among the Israelite people, who blatantly took advantage of one another, including those least likely to be able to defend themselves or their property (vv. 8–9). And yet, Micah's ethical message offers the exploited hope: God will act on their behalf, and those who have not kept covenant or Torah will be made to suffer the consequences of their unjust actions (vv. 3–5, 10).

Habakkuk 1:2–4; 2:6–20

Another passage that exposes the problem of social injustice among the Israelites is Habakkuk 1:2–4. This passage features the prophet Habakkuk's complaining to God about God's seemingly deaf ear toward his pleas (v. 2a), God's seeming inertia when he cries "violence" (v. 2b), and God's seeming insistence that Habakkuk see things he would rather not see (v. 3a). And what does Habakkuk see? Destruction, violence, strife, and contention (v. 3b), coupled with the experience of a failing judicial system whose ineffectiveness threatens the lives of the righteous and renders perverted decrees (v. 4).

---

[47]For land as a gift, see Numbers 34:2; 35:3, 8; 36:2; Deuteronomy 4:21, 38; 15:4; 19:10–14; 21:23; 24:4; 25:19; 26:1. For the relationship between "inheritance" and "land," see Deuteronomy 19:14. See also John Andrew Dearman, *Property Rights in the Eighth-Century Prophets,* 63; and Birch, *Let Justice Roll Down,* 261.

[48]In Hebrew, the word *hadar* could have the sense of either "land" or "freedom" (see L. Laberge, "Micah," in Raymond E. Brown, Joseph A. Fitzmyer and Roland E. Murphy, eds., *The New Jerome Biblical Commentary* [Englewood Cliffs, N. J.: Prentice Hall, 1990], 251). On the grounds of parallel structure, I argue that "land" is the better choice and seems to fit better with the idea of "houses" in verse 9a.

In 2:6–20, Habakkuk elaborates on the horrible vision to which he alluded in verse 3b. The passage consists of five woe statements that enumerate the injustices of some of the Israelites. They steal and cheat (v. 6), exploit others (vv. 6, 9), murder (v. 8), build towns and cities through corruption (v. 12), take advantage of others (v. 15), and trust in speechless, breathless idols (v. 19). Together, the five woes present a picture of how the ruthless ones have exerted their power to oppress others, to enhance their own projects unjustly, and to fall into the trap of idolatry. In the midst of such a bleak situation, Habakkuk proclaims:

> The cup in the LORD's right hand
> will come around to you,
> and shame will come upon
> your glory! (v. 16)

Iniquity will not be the final word; justice will prevail against those who have brought hardship and pain to others (vv. 7, 8, 11, 14, 17, 20).[49]

Social Injustice in Context

Looking at Isaiah 5:8–30; Jeremiah 5:20–29; 9:4–11; Amos 8:4–8; Micah 2:1–5, 8–9; and Habakkuk 1:2–4; 2:6–20, readers see that social injustice was a part of the tapestry of Israel's history. Most often, injustices were done to the least powerful and most vulnerable members of the community. Within these passages, the voice of the prophet resounds as it heralds a message of hope for those being made to suffer by their own people, but doom for those who persist in their incorrigible ways. Yet one problem remains: the prophets' description of God and how God plans to act to remedy the social injustices. Readers are confronted with a God who will bring about justice through violence (Jer. 5:29; 9:7–11), affecting not only human life but also nonhuman life and creation (see, e.g., Amos 8:9–14). In summary, the prophets' ethical message, which exposes, confronts, and promises to deal with social injustice, is a potent one, one that bears the markings of the historical, cultural, social, and theological assumptions of its day and that of its later editors and redactors.

Transgression, Ecology, and the Suffering of the Land

As seen in Amos 8:9–14, social injustice affected not only human life but also nonhuman life and, by extension, all creation. For Israel, sin and suffering were linked.[50] According to their worldview—understood and

---

[49]For further discussion, see Dempsey, *The Prophets*, 81–83.

[50]For further discussion on the relationship between sin and suffering as understood in Israel, see O. A. Piper, *IDB*, s.v. "Sin and Suffering," 4.

interpreted by their religious imagination, which interacted with their life experience—infidelity to God, the breaking of the covenant, and the forgetfulness and transgression of Torah led to punitive divine chastisement in the name of justice. Thus, in various prophetic texts, readers hear and see references to the suffering of the natural world, and specifically the suffering of the land, as a direct result of God's action. In essence, it was thought that God would or did strike the land in order to punish the people in an effort to reestablish justice and to woo them back to God through their repentance.[51] Hence, if the land experienced a drought or flood, crops would be destroyed and the people would suffer. Furthermore, when Israel did lose its land to foreign countries, this was also understood as either sanctioned or ordained by God because of the people's transgressions.[52]

The interrelatedness of social sin and the suffering of the natural world, particularly the suffering of the land, becomes apparent in selected texts from the prophetic writings of Isaiah, Hosea, Amos, Jeremiah, Joel, and Zephaniah pointing out to the people of their day that unless those who are responsible for injustice stop their unethical ways, the land will, in fact, suffer.[53] These prophets make a further point that the suffering of the land will result in the suffering and demise of civilization and the human race as well. Such a prophetic vision raises serious ethical issues that have demanded and continue to demand sharp ethical reflection and a strong response from contemporary readers, especially from among those of believing communities.

Before exploring this theme of the suffering of the land as it directly relates to the injustices caused by members of the human community, the word *'eres* needs consideration, since it is translated as both "earth" and "land" in the NRSV versions of the prophetic texts discussed in this section.

---

[51]See, e.g., Amos 4:6–12, especially verses 7–10.

[52]See, e.g., Jeremiah 1:14–16; 5:7–17, especially verses 15–17.

[53]The Isaiah, Amos, and Hosea texts in particular show that the land suffers for a variety of reasons, namely, (1) because of God's actions and judgments (see, e.g., Isa. 6:8–13; 13:9–13; 24; 34:8–12; Amos 8:4–8; cf. Jer. 4:28; 12:4; 23:10); (2) in response to human suffering caused by a "destroyer" (see Isa. 33:7–9); (3) as a direct result of human sinfulness (see, e.g., Hos. 4:1–3); and (4) as God's agent that God afflicts in order to persuade people to repent (see, e.g., Amos 4:6–10). Thus, in all instances the suffering of the land is in some way connected with human iniquity. In the cases of divine judgment where the land is afflicted, it is human sinfulness that sparks divine anger and becomes the motivation behind the divine judgment that is meant to chastise those guilty of injustices. Because land is central to the people's life, security, and livelihood, one sees that it often becomes God's agent for inflicting punishment, which, in turn, makes the land an "innocent victim" that suffers on account of others' misdeeds.

Toward an Understanding of the Hebrew Term 'eres

In the Old Testament, the Hebrew word *'eres* can mean "earth" when it is used in parallelism with the heavens or when a broad vision of life is intended.[54] Another interpretation of *'eres* is "land" when it is used in relation to a specific region, territory, or country.[55] A third interpretation of *'eres* is "ground."[56]

When dealing with those passages in Isaiah, specifically Isaiah 24, that directly speak of the suffering of the *'eres*, commentators generally translate *'eres* as "earth."[57] However, scholars interpret *'eres* in Hosea as the "land" that suffers.[58] Hence, the question arises, Which is the more appropriate interpretation of *'eres* given the discrepancy among commentators and the various dictionary definitions and nuances?

John D. W. Watts takes up the problem of the interpretation of *'eres* in his commentary on Isaiah. He points out that for the ancient people there was no ambiguity between "earth" and "land." Watts states that

> "Land" is the recognizable territory that one inhabits, visits, knows about. In the Near East, for Israel, "the land" was essentially the territory that faced the eastern Mediterranean Sea. This included Palestine/Syria and the wings in Mesopotamia in the Northeast and Egypt/Ethiopia in the South. The edges of Arabia come into view occasionally, as does Libya and distant Tarshish. This was *ha-'ares* "the civilised land," *ha-'adama* "the cultivatable land," or *tebel* "the world" to Israel.[59]

With respect to the way *'eres* is rendered in Isaiah 24, Watts concludes that "for translations (RSV, NIV, etc.) to render *ha-'ares* as 'the earth' in chapters 24—27 [of Isaiah] when they had rendered it 'the land' in previous chapters confuses the issue."[60] Thus, Watts interprets *'eres* as "land" in Isaiah

---

[54]For *'eres* as "earth" in parallelism with "heavens," see, e.g., Genesis 1:1; Psalm 113:6; Isaiah 1:2. See also Psalm 66:4; 135:7; and Isaiah 14:7, where *'eres* is also understood as "earth" in order to establish a broad sense of life. See also BDB, s.v. *'eres*, 1.

[55]For *'eres* as "land," see, e.g., 2 Kings 8:3; 2 Chronicles 34:7; and Amos 7:12. See also BDB, s.v. *'eres*, 2.

[56]For *'eres* as "ground," see, e.g., 2 Samuel 18:11; Daniel 9:15; and Amos 3:14. See also BDB, s.v. *'eres*, 3.

[57]See, e.g., Joseph Jensen, *Isaiah 1—39*, OTM 8 (Wilmington, Del.: Michael Glazier Press, 1984), 192–93, 195; and Oswalt, *The Book of Isaiah: Chapters 1—39*, 438–39. These commentators, among others, interpret *abela nabela ha ares* as "the earth mourns and withers."

[58]See, e.g., Wolff, *Hosea*, 65; and William R. Harper, *A Critical and Exegetical Commentary on Amos and Hosea*, ICC (Edinburgh: T. & T. Clark, 1979), 251. In Hosea 4:3, MT reads *te ebal ha-'ares*, "the land mourns." Both Wolff and Harper translate *ha-'ares* as "land," whereas in Isaiah 24:4, where *'eres* is also used with the verb *abal*, "to mourn," commentators translate *'eres* as "earth" (see n. 4).

[59]See John D. W. Watts, *Isaiah 1—33*, WordBC 24 (Waco, Tex.: Word Books, 1985), 316.

[60]Ibid.

24—27 and stresses that "the devastation, destruction, and shaking described in these chapters involves Palestine, Syria, Mesopotamia, and Egypt."[61] Furthermore, in Genesis 1:10 God calls the dry land "earth."

In light of the historical times of Isaiah, Hosea, Amos, and Micah, the arguments put forth by Watts, and the Genesis reference, I suggest that the renderings of *'eres* as "earth" and "land" are interchangeable, but that the more appropriate interpretation of *'eres* when used in conjunction with the idea of suffering is "land."

Isaiah 6:8–13 and 13:9–13

One first hears of the suffering of the land in Isaiah 6:8–13. In a dialogue between God and Isaiah, God commissions the prophet to go to his people and to perform a task that will incur suffering on the people. This suffering will be the dulling of their senses so that they will not be able to repent and turn back to God to be healed (vv. 9–10). To such a mandate, Isaiah responds with a question, "How long, O Lord?" (v. 11a). This question can be interpreted in two ways: "How long do I have to perform this task?" or "How long do the people have to suffer?" And God responds:

> "Until cities lie waste
> without inhabitant,
> and houses are without people,
> and the land is utterly desolate.
> Until the LORD sends everyone far away,
> and vast is the emptiness in the midst of the land.
> Even if a tenth part remain in it,
> it will be burned again,
> like a terebinth or an oak
> whose stump remains standing when it is felled."
> The holy seed is its stump. (vv. 11b–13)

Verses 11b–13 show the full extent of God's judgment upon the people. Nothing and no one will escape God's chastisement. And after all is said and done, what remains is the land, utterly desolate.

The question arises, Why are the people being divinely rebuked? Isaiah gives a glimpse into Judah's social condition in chapters 1—5. Members within the Israelite community have sinned; their sins are scarlet and red like crimson (Isa. 1:18); they have murdered, accepted bribes, neglected the orphan and widow (1:21–23), and have worshiped false gods (2:8).

---

[61]Ibid.

Some are proud and arrogant (2:11). Others oppress one another (3:5) as they join house to house and add field to field (5:8). Others call evil good and good evil (5:20). But worst of all, some have rejected Yahweh's instruction and have despised the word of the Holy One of Israel (5:24). Thus, certain members within the community have transgressed the law; they have broken covenant with God and with one another. Therefore, the community as a whole and the land will have to bear the consequences of divine retribution because God will not tolerate such unethical behavior. And the land will become utterly desolate (6:11–12). The land will be made to suffer because of human sinfulness.

Isaiah 13:9–13

In Isaiah 13, the oracle against Babylon, the prophet proclaims a stirring vision of judgment. Verses 9–16 describe the events that are to take place on the day of the Lord. In verses 9–13, Isaiah highlights specifically the universal and cosmic scope of God's wrath and intended chastisement:

> See, the day of the LORD comes,
> cruel, with wrath and fierce anger,
> to make the earth a desolation,
> and to destroy its sinners from it.
> For the stars of the heavens and their constellations
> will not give their light;
> the sun will be dark at its rising,
> and the moon will not shed its light.
> I will punish the world for its evil,
> and the wicked for their iniquity;
> I will put an end to the pride of the arrogant,
> and lay low the insolence of tyrants.
> I will make mortals more rare than fine gold,
> and humans than the gold of Ophir.
> Therefore I will make the heavens tremble,
> and the earth will be shaken out of its place,
> at the wrath of the LORD of hosts
> in the day of his fierce anger.

Oswalt points out that verses 9–13 "amplify the universal nature of the Lord's judgment. Once again, it is the pride of humanity which provokes this disaster (v. 11b), so that nature, too, is caught up in the catastrophic events."[62] Note that on the day of the Lord, not only will sinners be

---

[62]Oswalt, *The Book of Isaiah: Chapters 1—39*, 305.

destroyed but also *'eres*, "the land." The land will suffer divine wrath because of human sinfulness. Thus, "human sin has cosmic implications."[63] Given the content of Isaiah 6:8–13 and 13:9–13, the ethical and hermeneutical question that the texts evoke for contemporary readers is, Should the land be made to suffer on account of human sinfulness?

Isaiah 24

The theme of God's coming to chastise the people for their wickedness continues in Isaiah 24, the first of four chapters (24—27) that are often referred to as "the Isaiah Apocalypse." Clements states that these chapters "are designed to show how the fate of the nations, and especially of Israel among them, will ultimately be determined."[64]

Based on linguistic evidence that is too detailed to discuss in this chapter, one can divide Isaiah 24 into three main units: a judgment oracle (vv. 1–3); a vision of hope and sadness (vv. 4–20); and another judgment oracle (vv. 21–23).

In the first unit (vv. 1–3), the prophet proclaims that God is about "to lay waste the earth [*'eres*]" and make it desolate. God will "twist its surface and scatter its inhabitants" (v. 1). In verse 2, Isaiah catalogs six pairs of people who will be affected by the impending divine action. No class, religious group, or gender will escape God's judgment. In verse 3 the prophet reiterates his previous warning:

> The earth shall be utterly laid waste and utterly despoiled;
> for the LORD has spoken this word.

Collectively, verses 1–3 stress that both the land and all sorts of people are going to suffer, but the reason for the suffering is not yet made known.

The second unit (vv. 4–20) opens with the prophet's vision of the land's mourning and withering (v. 4). The repetitious use of the word *'eres* (fourteen times: vv. 4 [twice]; 5, 6 [twice]; 11, 13, 16, 17, 18, 19 [three times]; 20) in this unit and its focus on the land's suffering links verses 1–3 with 14–20. Through verbal and thematic repetition, Isaiah appeals to the hearts and minds of his audience, because even though land has an intrinsic value all its own, it is central to all of life's existence—plants, animals, and human beings alike. And for Israel, land is intimately linked to its historical and religious experience.

The Hebrew of verses 4–20 uses a series of perfect and converted perfect verb forms. With the exception of *'aberu*, "they have transgressed,"

---

[63]Ibid., 307.

[64]Ronald E. Clements, *Isaiah 1—39*, NCBC (Grand Rapids, Mich.: Eerdmans, 1980), 196. For further discussion on the background of Isaiah 24—27, see ibid., 196–200; Jensen, *Isaiah 1—39*, 190–92; Seitz, *Isaiah 1—39*, 172–79.

halepu, "they have violated," and *heperu*, "they have broken," in verse 5, I interpret all other perfects as present, which is consistent with prophetic vision.[65] Thus, verses 4–20 describe a picture of events that, in the prophet's mind, have already happened. Confident of his vision, Isaiah communicates it to his audience as if they are seeing the vision in the present. He makes the point that devastation is inevitable.

Verses 4–5 highlight the land's suffering and state the cause of such pain:

> The earth dries up and withers,
> the world languishes and withers;
> the heavens languish together with the earth.
> The earth lies polluted
> under its inhabitants;
> for they have transgressed laws,
> violated the statutes,
> broken the everlasting covenant.

The inhabitants, symbolized by the various groups cataloged in verse 2, have sinned. The land mourns, withers, and languishes because some people have transgressed Torah, violated the law, and broken the everlasting covenant.[66] The imagery in verse 4 also suggests a severe drought.

Holladay notes that the phrase "and the [land] lies polluted under its inhabitants" in verse 5 is a phrase that "refers specifically to Numbers 35:33. There it is stated that the blood shed by a murderer pollutes the land. So Isaiah 24:5 implies that the earth is polluted because of the heavy toll of murder it has sustained."[67]

To what covenant the phrase "they...have broken the everlasting covenant" in verse 5 refers is debated among scholars. Otto Kaiser and Christopher R. Seitz argue in favor of the Noachic covenant.[68] Clements sees the possibility that the "everlasting covenant" could be referring to the Mosaic covenant in light of the references to the "Torah" and "law."[69] The Mosaic covenant would mean that the vision is meant only for the Israelites. The word *tebel*, "world," in verse 4 suggests a more cosmic perspective.

---

[65]When used in prophetic oracles, the *qatal* verb form can be interpreted as both a prophetic perfect (P. Joüon, *A Grammar of Biblical Hebrew*, trans. T. Muraoka, Subsidia Biblica 14/II [Rome: Pontifical Biblical Institute, 1991], s112h) and a *perfectum confidentiae* (E. Kautzsch and A. E. Cowley, eds., *Gesenius' Hebrew Grammar*, 2d ed. [Oxford: Clarendon, 1910], s106n).

[66]See Leviticus 26:27–33, 40–45.

[67]W. L. Holladay, *Isaiah: Scroll of a Prophetic Heritage* (Grand Rapids, Mich.: Eerdmans, 1978), 195–96.

[68]For further discussion on the "everlasting covenant," see Otto Kaiser, *Isaiah 13—39: A Commentary* (Philadelphia: Westminster Press, 1974), 183; and Seitz, *Isaiah 1—39*, 179–84.

[69]Clements, *Isaiah 1—39*, 202–4.

In addition to establishing an "everlasting covenant" with Noah in Genesis 9:16, Yahweh establishes one with Abraham (Gen. 17:13) and promises to do so with Isaac (Gen. 17:19). David also shares in an everlasting covenant with God (2 Sam. 23:5), as do the Israelites in the time of Ezekiel (Ezek. 16:60) and in Jeremiah's day (Jer. 32:40). They shall be "Yahweh's" people, and "Yahweh" will be their God (Jer. 32:38). Finally, the Sabbath rest is designated as an "everlasting covenant" to act as a sign between Yahweh and the Israelites (Ex. 31:16; compare Lev. 24:8).

Taking into account the different scholarly arguments and the variety of biblical references to the "everlasting covenant," and in the context of the phrase as it appears in verses 4–5, it seems that the "everlasting covenant" does not refer to a single, specific covenant, but rather more broadly to a cosmic covenant that God has made with all people and all of creation.[70] Thus, the inhabitants who break the everlasting covenant are both Israelites and non-Israelites—the inhabitants of the land who live in the world. And the land is made to suffer because of some people's sinfulness.

Verse 6 is a pivotal verse that looks backward to verses 4–5 and forward to verses 7–12. Beginning with the conjunction "therefore," Isaiah pronounces the consequences of humankind's transgressions:

> Therefore a curse devours the earth,
> and its inhabitants suffer for their guilt;
> therefore the inhabitants of the earth dwindled,
> and few people are left.

Once again, the land suffers.

Verses 7–12 expand on verse 6. In verses 7–12 the prophet outlines very clearly what is to take place as a result of the divine curse and chastisement. Because the land is cursed, the "wine dries up," "the vine languishes," and "all the merry-hearted sigh" (v. 7). The curse of the land affects its vegetation, which in turn affects the people. The image of the wine drying up and the vine languishing harks back to verse 4 where the land mourns and the world and the heavens languish together with the earth. The imagery of suffering associated with sin pervades Isaiah's message.

Verses 8–9 pick up the dispiritedness of the people expressed in verse 7. Festivities, normally celebrated when the vintage is completed, come to a halt.[71] There is no music, no wine, no song.

In verses 10–12 the progression of the curse and chastisement mentioned in verse 6 continues. The "city of chaos is broken down,"

---

[70]For further discussion on the cosmic covenant, see Robert Murray, *The Cosmic Covenant: Biblical Themes of Justice and Peace, and the Integrity of Creation* (London: Sheed & Ward, 1992), 1–22.

[71]For further discussion on the cessation of the vintage festivities, see Clements, *Isaiah 1—39*, 202.

houses are shut up as people bemoan the lack of wine, "all joy has reached its eventide," and "the gladness of the earth is banished." The city is left desolate, and even the gates are "battered into ruins." Thus, human sinfulness now affects not only the land but also civilization as a whole.

Verse 13 is a summary of verses 4–12. It begins with the phrase "for thus it shall be on the earth and among the nations." Here the prophet links the land and the people together. The shift from the prophetic perfect in verses 4–12 to the imperfect in verse 13 serves as a shift in time and focus. The vision of devastation (vv. 4–12) within the prophetic proclamation (vv. 1–24) has come to an end, and Isaiah now states that what he has envisioned for the people in verses 4–12 will indeed come to pass. In order to intensify his message and hold his audience's attention, Isaiah uses two similes from the natural world common to the people of his day. The future verb tense expressed in verse 13 is similar to that in verses 1–3. Thus, the message that Isaiah proclaims and the vision that he describes to the people in the midst of his message will indeed come to pass.

Following a descriptive vision of cosmic catastrophe comes a vision of hope in verses 14–16a. These verses describe a group of jubilant people who are joyful over God. Isaiah does not name them or suggest who "they" are who lift up their voices and sing for joy. Commentators offer a variety of suggestions.[72] In the context of verses 1–15, it seems that the jubilant ones are the righteous among all the people who remain faithful to their relationship with God and with one another. Perhaps these are the few in verse 6 who remain after all else is cursed and chastised. Perhaps they are the "remnant." Perhaps the ones in verses 14–15 who are jubilant over God's majesty are those who were once oppressed and sinned against who now witness the demise of their oppressors—the sinners. But one problem still remains. How can the people sing when the land has been devastated and people are wasted because of their sinfulness? Should not their song be a song of mourning as well as joy?

The prophet laments in verses 16b–20. Unlike the jubilant ones who sing for joy in verses 14–16a, Isaiah sings a mourning song (vv. 16b–20) that begins, "I pine away, I pine away. Woe is me!" (v. 16b) He laments how treacherously the treacherous deal; he grieves that terror, the pit, and the snare are upon the inhabitants of the land (v. 17) and that there shall be no escape (v. 18). Finally, very poignantly, Isaiah mourns for the land in verses 19–20:

---

[72]See, e.g., Clements, *Isaiah 1—39*, 204; G. B. Gray, *A Critical and Exegetical Commentary on the Book of Isaiah I—XXVII*, ICC (Edinburgh: T. & T. Clark, 1912), 417.

The earth is utterly broken,
the earth is torn asunder,
the earth is violently shaken.
The earth staggers like a drunkard,
it sways like a hut;
its transgression lies heavy upon it,
and it falls, and will not rise again.

The land—the earth, *'eres*—created and named by God, *'eres* who has cared for and welcomed so many people, *'eres* who is home to everything living, is on its last leg and is destined to fall, never to rise, all because of humankind's sinfulness.

Verses 21–23 are a judgment statement. The phrase "on that day the LORD will punish" (v. 21) signals a new unit. For the prophet, what he envisioned for the people has come to a close, but for the people, the vision is about to unfold. The day of the Lord is coming; God's justice is about to take place (vv. 1–3, 4–20, 21–22), beginning with the host of heaven in the heights and "the kings of the earth" who, because of their office, have the responsibility of ensuring justice among the inhabitants of the land (see Mic. 3:1–12). Finally, in the cosmic setting of verse 23, Isaiah proclaims that it is Yahweh, a God of justice, who will reign in the land.

In summary, Isaiah 24 is a prophetic proclamation that contains a vision. While offering a glimmer of hope and joy (vv. 14–16a), Isaiah 24 reveals a vivid picture of suffering and describes the gradual demise of the land, the people, and their civilization. Isaiah 24 celebrates the justice of God, who will not tolerate injustice. Finally, Isaiah 24 gives direct evidence that the suffering of the land is linked to human sinfulness. Despite its hopeful last verse (v. 21), the passage leaves readers with two nagging questions: How long must the land suffer? and, Why must the land be made to suffer?

Isaiah 33:7–9; 34:8–12

In addition to Isaiah 6:11–13; 13:9–13; and 24, two other passages in Isaiah speak of the suffering of the land. Isaiah 33:7–9 is a lament describing the distress that an enemy nation is causing the Israelites.[73] Oswalt comments: "Verses 7–9 depict a situation where all hope is lost. The heroes cannot help, nor can the diplomats. The destroyer will not abide by his

---

[73]The identity of the enemy nation in Isaiah 33:7–9 is not identified. It is most likely Babylon but may be Assyria. For further discussion, see Clements, *Isaiah 1—39*, 265.

agreements (cf. 33:1) but comes on for destruction. Thus everyone mourns, even the land itself."[74] As in Isaiah 6:11–13; 13:9–13; and 24, the suffering of the land, in this case, its mourning and languishing, is associated with human wickedness (33:8).

In Isaiah 34:8–12 the prophet describes another instance of the land suffering (v. 9). In the context of a judgment on the nations (34:1–17), the focus of verses 8–12 is Edom. On the day when Yahweh comes to judge Edom for all its wicked deeds against Judah, Edom's streams "shall be turned into pitch," "her soil into sulfur," and "her land shall become burning pitch" (v. 9) that will be unquenchable (v. 10). Again, the suffering of the land is associated with human sinfulness.[75]

Hosea 4:1–3

Hosea also speaks of the suffering of the land in relation to human sinfulness. The most striking passage is Hosea 4:1–3, a judgment speech (a *rib*) against Israel. In verses 1–2, Hosea outlines the grievances that Yahweh has against Israel:

> There is no faithfulness or loyalty,
> and no knowledge of God in the land.
> Swearing, lying, and murder,
> and stealing and adultery break out;
> bloodshed follows bloodshed.

The conjunction "therefore" in verse 3 begins the description of the land's suffering. Implied is that the suffering will be the result of divine judgment that will take the form of a drought.

> Therefore the land mourns,
> and all who live in it languish;
> together with the wild animals
> and the birds of the air,
> and even the fish of the sea are perishing.

Like Isaiah, Hosea draws a connection between the suffering of the land and human sinfulness. But this time not only the land is affected but also the animals and fish, who, like the land, have done nothing to deserve such painful chastisement.

---

[74]Oswalt, *The Book of Isaiah: Chapters 1—39*, 595.
[75]See also Isaiah 42:14–17 for the suffering of the land in relation to divine chastisement for idolatry.

Amos 4:6–10; 8:4–8

Two passages in the book of Amos that associate the suffering of the land with divine chastisement of humanity are Amos 4:6–10 and 8:4–8. In Amos 4:6–10, God is portrayed as one who upbraids the Israelites for their unwillingness to repent despite the divine calamities that befall them. In an effort to get Israel to return to Yahweh, Yahweh withholds the rain. This causes a portion of the land to dry up (Am. 4:7).

In verses 9–10 the prophet lists all the punitive acts that Yahweh inflicted on Israel in the past, yet Israel did not repent. Each of these punitive acts involved some sort of suffering by the land and other elements of nature. Yahweh struck Israel with "blight and mildew"; gardens and vineyards were laid waste; locusts devoured the fig and almond trees (v. 9). A pestilence came upon the people; young men were killed by the sword; horses were carried away; even unpleasant odors were brought upon them. Yet Israel did not repent and return to Yahweh. Of importance here is the fact that nature is affected by Yahweh's punitive deeds because Israel is stubborn. And the question arises, Should the land and the gifts of nature be used to incur chastisement?

In 8:4–8, Amos enumerates the injustices that the Israelites commit against one another (vv. 4–6). In verse 8, Amos poses two rhetorical questions that draw attention to the land and the mourning of its inhabitants. And the message is clear: "The presupposition here, as in Hos 4:1–3, is that anyone in Israel who tampers with the just orders of life draws the earth and its inhabitants into perdition at the same time."[76]

Jeremiah 7:16–20; 12:4; 23:9–11

In the book of Jeremiah, the theme of human transgression and its connection to the suffering of the land expands to include not only the human community but also other nonhuman forms of life. Distinctive among the passages discussed thus far is the theme of the land's mourning heard in Jeremiah 12:4 and 23:9–11.

Jeremiah 7:16–20 is a personal address to Jeremiah from God that begins with a *casus pendens*, "as for you," followed by three negative divine commands: "do not pray for this people"; "do not raise a cry or prayer on their behalf"; and "do not intercede with me." God's patience with the people has been exhausted, and therefore Jeremiah's intercession on their behalf will be pointless, because God has taken a stand: "I will not hear you" (v. 16). In verse 17, God confronts Jeremiah with a rhetorical question that leads into a lawsuit speech in verses 18–19, where God indicts the

---

[76]Hans Walter Wolff, *Joel and Amos,* trans. W. Janzen, S. D. McBride, Jr., and C. A. Muenchow, Hermeneia (Philadelphia: Fortress Press, 1977), 329.

Judahites for apostasy and idolatry. Provoked, God issues a judgment statement against the people in response to their infidelity:

> My anger and my wrath shall be poured out on this place, on human beings and animals, on the trees of the field and the fruit of the ground; it will burn and not be quenched. (v. 20)

Breach of covenant fidelity on the part of some Judahites will have devastating effects on life. To readers the text suggests that human beings, the animals, the trees, and the fruit on the ground will be made to suffer the consequences of divine anger and wrath because of human transgression.

In 12:4, Jeremiah complains to God about the drought that has caused the land to mourn (metaphorically), grass to wither, and animals and birds to be swept away:

> How long will the land mourn,
> and the grass of every field wither?
> For the wickedness of those who live in it
> the animals and birds are swept away,
> and because people said, "He is blind to our ways."

As in Jeremiah 7:16–20, the text suggests to readers an inherent connection between the unethical ways of human beings and the suffering of the natural world.

Jeremiah 23:9–11 picks up the theme of the land's mourning heard in 12:4. In verses 9–11, Jeremiah reflects on his own personal condition (v. 9) and then that of his surroundings:

> For the land is full of adulterers;
> because of the curse the land mourns,
> and the pastures of the wilderness are dried up. (v. 10a)

Among the adulterers in the land are the prophet and the priest, both "ungodly" (v. 11). Drought, understood as a means of divine chastisement for human infidelity to covenant and Torah, has caused the land to mourn and the pastures to dry up. The text suggests a direct relationship between human transgression and the suffering of the land.

Joel 1:15–18

The image of the suffering of the natural world is also found in the book of Joel. One example is 1:15–18. Joel shouts out a cry of terror, "Alas for the day!" (v. 15a). He warns his listeners in Jerusalem and Judah of the coming of the day of the Lord, which will be a day of destruction coming directly from God (v. 15b). This day of doom will be a time of calamity caused by locusts and a drought, both of which would be understood that day as God's punitive judgment on the people. Crops will fail; granaries will collapse; and the animals cry out and go about dazed for lack of pasture (vv. 17–18). Although no specific reason for the impending time of devastation is given in this unit, 2:12–14 suggests that the people have not been in right relationship with their God and thus will be the recipients of God's chastisement, which will have negative effects on the natural world and will, in turn, affect the people.

Zephaniah 1:2–6

One final text that suggests a relationship between human transgression and the suffering of the natural world with the land implied is Zephaniah 1:2–6. In these verses, God through Zephaniah warns Judah of impending judgment that will result in terrible devastation. God pledges to utterly sweep away everything from the face of the earth: humans, animals, birds of the air, fish of the sea. The wicked will stumble, and humanity will be cut off from the face of the earth. Additionally, God cut off from Judah every remnant of Baal, along with the name of the idolatrous priests (vv. 2–4). The reason for such divine wrath is clear from verses 4–6: idolatry. Breach of covenant relationship on the part of human beings reaps repercussions that devastate not only humanity but the natural world as well.

The Suffering of the Land and the Natural World in Context

Selected texts from a variety of prophets highlight human transgression and the suffering of the land in particular and the natural world in general. For contemporary readers the texts suggest three main ethical and theological points. First, the God of the cosmos who created and sustains all living matter will not tolerate injustice, especially when human beings oppress one another. God does chastise the wicked and thus gives hope to the oppressed, but the chastisement comes in such a way that it affects the land. This situation is problematic and raises further ethical issues with respect to how God is portrayed in the prophetic texts. Second, sinfulness on the part of some human beings does affect the rest of the natural world. Third, there is an intricate relationship, an everlasting *berit*, "covenant," that exists between God and humanity, the land, and all living matter. When that covenant and its responsibilities are not understood, or when the covenant is broken, the vulnerable, the poor, the innocent, and the land suffer. Power, control, and domination are achieved at the expense of the most vulnerable. Hence, there is a systemic connection between the oppression of people and the oppression of this land, one of the many vulnerable ones on the planet.

In their reflections on the conditions of the earth, contemporary theologians are drawing attention to the destruction and loss of our rain forests and woods that not only result in the loss of land but also lead to the extinction of many animal species driven from their natural habitats. Another issue is the continuous use of the land for agricultural purposes without giving it a rest, which, in the end, strips the land of its ability to replenish and restore itself and thus causes it to become infertile. The ozone layer continues to be depleted; acid rain affects the land, its crops and plants, water supplies, and consequently, humans, animals, plants, and plant life. Lorna Green raises the question of why this is happening and offers a bold response: "Why is all this happening? Because of us. We human beings are the cause of the agony of the earth."[77]

Finally, Janice and Donald Kirk point out a three-way relationship, suggestive of covenant, that exists among God, human beings, and creation: The natural world is the arena God chose to develop life for a divine purpose. In this arena a three-way arrangement connects God, humans, and creation. God created and oversees the earth and its inhabitants. The creation reveals God and supports life on earth. Humans reach out to God as we live in the creation. The participants are inseparably linked. If we turn away from God or tamper with our connections with the creation, we suffer from a godless life, and the creation suffers with us.[78]

In summary, Isaiah's vision in 24:4–5 is no longer a vision, and the mourning of the land and the animals that Jeremiah and Joel speak about is no longer metaphorical. The planet and all its inhabitants and life forms are suffering in large part because some members of the human community have violated their right relationship with creation, tipped the balance, and acted unjustly and unethically. When read in a contemporary socioecological context, the texts of the prophets mentioned in this section offer readers a disturbing picture that calls for an ethical response that can no longer be avoided. Thus, in the rereading of these selected texts comes a new awareness that could inspire a change of heart and ways among human beings so that all creation might flourish.

---

[77]Lorna Green, *Earth Age: A New Vision of God, the Human, and the Earth* (Mahwah, N.J.: Paulist Press, 1994), 17. Douglas John Hall (*The Steward: A Biblical Symbol Come of Age* [Grand Rapids, Mich.: Eerdmans, 1990], 193) concurs with Green and adds that "nature suffers, not when human beings are willing and doing what, in God's intention, they are meant to do, but when they sin!" For further discussion, see Roger S. Gottlieb, ed., *This Sacred Earth: Religion, Nature, Environment* (New York: Routledge, 1996); and Norman C. Habel, *The Land is Mine,* OBT (Minneapolis: Fortress Press, 1995), 134–48.

[78]Janice E. Kirk and Donald R. Kirk, *Cherish the Earth: The Environment and Scripture* (Scottdale, Pa.: Herald Press, 1993), 44.

Chapter 5

Ethics That Challenge,
Images That Disturb

The literature of Israel's prophets reflects to a certain degree the beliefs and experiences of the Israelite people, who struggled to be faithful to their God. The Israelites were a people chosen by God to live in covenant with God, and a people to whom God had entrusted Torah, which they were called to embrace. In their early years as a tribal people, the Israelites came to realize that their election was because God loved them and that this God was faithful to the divine promises made to their ancestors. They also knew that the essence of the law was love, a love that demanded a single-heartedness with respect to their relationship with their God and the living out of God's ways.[1] Both covenant and Torah called them to a relational, responsible, and ethical way of life for the sake of the common good of all creation. And while they basked in God's love and delight, they also perceived themselves to be living in the shadow of God's wrath. Thus, if they were faithful, God would bless and reward them, but if they were unfaithful, God would curse and punish them.[2] The book of Deuteronomy in particular reflects these ideas and beliefs, and from this book, and the deuteronomistic history as a whole, one can extrapolate a theology of love and a theology of retribution that appears in the books of the Prophets.[3]

---

[1] See Deuteronomy 7:6–11 and 10:12–16.
[2] See especially Deuteronomy 28.
[3] For further discussion on the idea of retribution as it pertains to deed and consequence, and as it is understood within the deuteronomistic history of Israel, see Horst Dietrich Preuss, *Old Testament Theology*, vol. 1 (Louisville, Ky.: Westminster John Knox Press, 1995), 184–94.

The Israelite people as a unified nation and then as two divided kingdoms were also a people who lived with the constant threat of military invasion from neighboring enemies, particularly the Assyrians and Babylonians, each of whom contributed to the fall of the Northern and Southern Kingdoms, respectively. In addition to their struggle to remain secure in the land that God had given them as a gift, the Israelites struggled with internal conflicts arising from a wide variety of injustices, many of which seem to have gone unchecked and unresolved.

Furthermore, by the time of the prophet Hosea in the eighth century B.C.E., covenant and covenant language had become associated with marriage and marital images. This is also seen later in the writings of Ezekiel and, to some extent, in the book of Jeremiah. God, then, was portrayed as not only a male deity but also the husband of Israel, which was imaged as female and wife.[4]

Thus, the texts of the Prophets reflect past traditions and beliefs of the community. These traditions and beliefs were historically, socially, and culturally conditioned by their own lived experience. The following three descriptions of God are found in various texts of the Prophets: (1) a God of punitive justice; (2) a warrior God; and (3) a faithful God whose covenant partner is often guilty of harlotry and whoredom. These descriptions reflect Israel's historical situation, which seems to have colored the people's religious imagination.

Many of Israel's prophets use vivid images of God as well as gender-specific language and images for Israel in their proclamations to make an ethical point. These images suggest a certain degree of violence that is legitimized by the biblical text and by the fact that the proclamations are understood to be "prophetic" and "ethical." In an effort to bring to the surface points and questions that call for further hermeneutical reflection and comment, this chapter explores the images of a God of punitive justice and a warrior God, and gender-specific language as it is applied negatively to Israel/Jerusalem.

Considering the "Just-ness" of God's Justice

Within the books of Ezekiel, Amos, Nahum, Zephaniah, Lamentations, and Baruch is a description of a God who promises to act with divine justice to punish those among the chosen ones who are guilty of infidelity and injustices. For those who are victims of injustice, this God offers a sense of hope; there will be an end to their misery. However, this image of a God of punitive justice can also be rather disturbing because of the

---

[4]A classic example of such imagery can be found in Hosea 2:16–20.

expression of violence that is attributed to God and God's justice and its relationship to the preaching and ethical message of the prophets.

Heard and read in the context of a contemporary global community that suffers with and from the reality of violence and its myriad forms of expression, the prophets' ethical message affirming a God whose justice is punitive and violent is a message that cannot go unexplored.

Ezekiel 7:1–9

Ezekiel 7:1–9 is part of one of Ezekiel's greatest poems (vv. 1–27). This passage consists of two units (vv. 2–4 and vv. 5–9) that describe a vision of divinely planned impending disaster. The first unit opens with a comment by Ezekiel (v. 1) and is followed by a prophecy of divine judgment uttered by God through Ezekiel (vv. 2–4). In this vision, God reveals to the prophet what he must say to the people, namely, that the end has come for the land and for them (v. 2). In verses 3–4, God catalogs what God plans to do to the people. God will let loose divine anger upon them, judge them according to their ways, punish them for all their abominations, spare no one, and show no pity. And all of this is because of the people's abominations—their wicked ways (v. 3) and their apostasy and idolatry (v. 4).[5] The narrative phrase "Then you shall know that I am the LORD" (v. 4b) expresses God's power and sovereignty over the land and the people. Israel will come to know God as "Lord" through God's anger and God's violent, merciless deeds of judgment.

The sentiment of divine wrath continues in verses 5–9. Following a traditional messenger statement (v. 5a), God through Ezekiel reveals that disaster after disaster comes and that, indeed, an end—*the* end—has come (v. 6). Doom has come to the people (v. 7). God then announces a second time the divine judgment plan (vv. 8–9). These two verses are similar to, yet distinct from, verses 3–4. God, who promises to "let loose" divine anger (v. 3), will now "pour out" divine wrath upon the people (v. 8). And the God who promises to punish the people "for" their ways (v. 4) will now punish them "according to" their ways. Hence, there is a subtle intensification in verses 8–9 of God's anger and chastisement that was first expressed in verses 3–4. This sense of intensification also occurs in the short narrative phrase that closes the unit: "Then you shall know that it is I the LORD who strike" (v. 9b). Here God assumes personal ownership for the violent deeds of judgment about to befall the people.

---

[5]I argue that in verse 3 "abominations" refers to the people's wicked ways (see Jer. 7:10), and in verse 4 it refers to the people's idolatry and apostasy (see Jer. 4:1; 7:30; 8:1–18; and Ezek. 6:14). Thus, the word has a double meaning in these two verses.

It is obvious from verses 3–4 that the people have transgressed Torah and violated their covenant with God. Such deeds warrant the implementation of justice. As the text stands, however, it reflects a theology of retribution and heralds an ethical message that sanctions the use of violence to correct infractions and injustices. It also raises the question, How ethical are the ethics of Israel's prophets?[6]

Amos 9:1–4

The theme of divine wrath continues in Amos 9:1–4, the fifth of a series of vision reports in the book of Amos. In this passage Amos tells about a vision that concerns God's judgment on the kingdom of Jeroboam. In this vision God is depicted as one who authorizes power to be used destructively and promises to use it personally in the same way:

> Strike the capitals until the thresholds shake,
> and shatter them on the heads of all the people;
> and those who are left I will kill with the sword;
> not one of them shall flee away,
> not one of them shall escape. (v. 1)

Verses 2–4 describe God's inescapable wrath; the people will be made to suffer. God vows to snatch them from whatever hiding place they choose as an escape. If they dig into Sheol, God's hand will take them; if they climb up to heaven, God's hand will bring them down (v. 2); if they hide on top of Carmel, God will search them out and take them; if they hide at the bottom of the sea, God will command the sea-serpent to bite them (v. 3); if they go into captivity in front of their enemies, God will command the sword, and it shall kill them (v. 4a). God's intentions are stated clearly:

> I will fix my eyes on them
> for harm and not for good. (v. 4b)

Hence, "the omnipresent sovereignty of Yahweh becomes an ominous and terrible reality that lends to his decree of punishment an absolute finality."[7] God has passed a legal verdict on Israel for its transgressions, and judgment will be punitive and intentional.[8]

---

[6] See Ezekiel 9:1–11 for a gruesome narrative that outlines divine judgment on those in Jerusalem who are guilty of idolatry.

[7] James Luther Mays, *Amos,* OTL (Philadelphia: Westminster Press, 1969), 154.

[8] For another gripping description of God's punishment that affects both human and nonhuman life, see Amos 4:6–13.

Nahum 1:1–11

One of the most vivid and horrifying pictures of the God of justice appears in Nahum 1:1–11. Without reservation, Nahum proclaims that God is a "jealous and avenging God," one who is "wrathful," who "takes vengeance on his adversaries" (v. 2), and who does not clear the guilty (v. 3). This God is the storm God who rebukes the sea, dries up all the rivers, and makes the flowers die, the mountains quake, the hills melt, and the earth heave (vv. 3–5). Divine protection is extended to those who take refuge in God, but God will "make a full end of his adversaries, and will pursue his enemies into darkness" (v. 8). With the proclamation of this vision, Nahum warns his listeners about Israel's God, and one can see from the text that God's justice against the enemies will be punitive.

Zephaniah 1:14–18

With graphic detail, Zephaniah describes the great day of the Lord that is drawing near. This day will be a day of wrath, distress, anguish, ruin, devastation, darkness, trumpet blast, and battle cry against the fortified cities (vv. 14–16). Following this description comes the voice of God through Zephaniah that assures the people that divine judgment will be punitive and cosmic—the whole earth will be consumed by God's wrath (vv. 17–18). Both the text and the prophet's proclamation make clear that the great day of the Lord will be a punitive one because of the people's sinfulness (vv. 17–18).

Lamentations 4:1–20

The image of God as the one who punishes reaches a blistering crescendo in Lamentations 4:1–20, a poem that describes the desperation and anguish of the Judahites after the fall of Jerusalem, the temple, and the Southern Kingdom in 587 B.C.E. In this poem the prophet tells of the people's suffering, which he relates against the backdrop of earlier, more prosperous days. Such a contrast accentuates the present experience of devastation.

The prophet begins with an expression of lament:

How the gold has grown dim,
how the pure gold is changed!
The sacred stones lie scattered
at the head of every street. (v. 1)

In the verses that follow, the plight of the Judahites unfolds. Zion's children, once worth their weight in gold, are now reckoned as earthen pots (v. 2). And although the animals are able to feed and care for their young, the Judahites cannot:

The tongue of the infant sticks
to the roof of its mouth for thirst;
the children beg for food,
but no one gives them anything. (v. 4)

Moreover, those accustomed to palatal delicacies and fine clothes now starve and "cling to ash heaps" (v. 5). Stately princes, once pictures of beauty, are now gaunt and shriveled (vv. 7–8). Women have boiled their own children for food (v. 10). A people defiled and repulsed (vv. 14–15), they hoped against hope for a nation to save them (v. 17), only to be overcome by their pursuers (vv. 18–19), who even captured their king, Zedekiah—the "Lord's anointed," the "breath" of their life—after he tried to escape from Jerusalem at the time of the last great siege (see 2 Kings 25:3–6). This invasion of an enemy nation through the gates of Jerusalem took "the kings of the earth" by surprise (v. 12) because, in accordance with Zion theology, who would have ever thought that God's holy city would be annihilated!

The prophet attributes the people's pain and the demise of Jerusalem to a chastisement that was greater than the punishment of Sodom (v. 6), and one that God had inflicted:

The LORD gave full vent to his wrath;
he poured out his hot anger,
and kindled a fire in Zion
that consumed its foundations. (v. 11; see also v. 16)

The reason for the vented wrath and heated anger that caused such pain, starvation, and the demise of a kingdom was sin—the sins of the prophets and the iniquities of the priests (v. 13).

The text portrays a God of justice who has acted with justice; those who have sinned have received their just deserts. The righteous whose blood has been shed have been vindicated (v. 13). But what about the infants, the children—those who are the most vulnerable among the Judahites—who are made to bear the consequences of divine justice as a response to others' transgressions? The prophet reports the sad details but does not question God's punitive justice. Such resignation suggests to contemporary readers the question, How ethical is the prophets' message? The text also serves as a reminder that many traditions helped to shape the biblical material now in its final canonical form. These traditions, especially the deuteronomistic theology of retribution that this text reflects, invite further consideration and comment if one is to come to an understanding of God as a God of justice and not a God of historical interpretations and theological constructs of an ancient world.

Baruch 1:15—2:10

The theme of divine justice continues in Baruch 1:15—2:10. In this passage, Baruch is requested by the Judahite officials and exiles to read aloud from the scroll that they are sending him. This is to be done publicly on feast days and is to serve as a sign of their true contrite spirit and their firm purpose to change their ways (vv. 13–14). Baruch 1:15—2:10 contains the content of the scroll that expresses the people's sentiments.

The passage opens with the community's affirming God's justice: "The Lord our God is in the right" (1:15), followed by a detailed description of the people's transgressions, inclusive of apostasy (1:22). The community next comments on how God carried out the divine threat spoken against them. Here it becomes clear that in the people's minds, they were deserving of having the divine threat become a reality because they were guilty of sin and did not entreat the favor of God by turning away from the thoughts of their wicked hearts (2:8). They neglected to obey God's voice and failed to walk in God's ways (2:10). A second time they affirm that "the Lord our God is in the right" (2:6) with respect to God's punitive justice as a response to their transgressions.

This passage suggests how the deuteronomistic theology of retribution may have influenced a community, and how they seem to have interpreted their historical and social reality of exile through this theological lens. Moreover, because this passage is considered to be "prophetic," it has the potential to influence negatively a reader's understanding of God and God's justice if certain elements are not unpacked and carefully considered in relation to their historical and theological contexts within the ancient Near Eastern world.[9]

God's Justice in Context

The biblical texts examined in this section point out that Israel's God is a God of justice who will not tolerate injustice and who will act with justice to counteract and to correct transgressions against covenant and Torah. The description of God's justice, however, reflects certain theological principles and constructs generic to the ancient world. Because these principles and constructs continue to influence people's thinking about God and their understanding of God's justice, the texts studied in this section call for a contemporary hermeneutical assessment that recognizes the variety of theological ethics and perspectives represented in the writings of the prophets. Indeed, the prophet Hosea reminds believers past and present that the flip side of God's justice is God's compassion:

---

[9]For further study on the deuteronomistic theology of retribution and the connection between deed and consequence, see Preuss, *Old Testament Theology,* vol. 1, 184–94.

My heart recoils within me;
my compassion grows warm and tender.
I will not execute my fierce anger;
I will not again destroy Ephraim;
for I am God and no mortal,
the Holy One in your midst,
and I will not come in wrath. (11:8c–9)

Moreover, God's justice will not be punitive in the ways that the human community would either expect or enforce.

The Ethics of Israel's God as Divine Warrior

One common motif that appears in the writings of the prophets is God as a divine warrior. This metaphor for God reflects the lived social and historical realities of Israel, whose people lived under constant threat and in the midst of military invasion from enemy countries and empires.

The idea of war and the metaphor of God as warrior have been topics of scholarly conversation for some time. In two recent works, one by Susan Niditch titled *War in the Hebrew Bible: A Study in the Ethics of Violence*,[10] and a second by John A. Woods, *Perspectives on War in the Bible*,[11] the topic of war in the ancient Israelite world is explored extensively. Both authors examine various theories of war and war motifs present in the Old Testament/Hebrew Scriptures, and both explore the idea of *herem*, or "the ban," that is associated with war texts.

Under the *herem*, all human beings among those defeated were devoted to destruction. Specifically, as in Numbers 21:2–3, the Israelites pledge their enemies to God as a promise for God's support in battle and of divine support for their military successes. The deuteronomic writers placed this ban in a "just war" context. Niditch points out that "anthropologists of a Marxian or cultural materialistic persuasion suggest that ideologies such as the ban as God's justice, in fact, mask the true goals of combat and killing in war—namely the desire to take the enemies' land or goods or women in order better to assure the prospering, perhaps the survival, of one's own group."[12] Niditch concludes that the attitudes of war in the Hebrew Scriptures are "as old as human culture itself and as complex as human thought, linking our earliest ancestors with ourselves and our neighbors' cultures with our own" as we struggle between "compassion

---

[10]See Susan Niditch, *War in the Hebrew Bible: A Study in the Ethics of Violence* (New York: Oxford University Press, 1993).

[11]See John A. Woods, *Perspectives on War in the Bible* (Macon, Ga.: Mercer University Press, 1998).

[12]See Niditch, *War in the Hebrew Bible*, 127.

and enmity."[13] Woods points out further that the "realism of the Bible" is apparent insofar as it recognizes that people are born into a world in which power is not evenly distributed. If one desires to change that distribution, some sort of conflict will ultimately be inevitable.[14]

With respect to the image of God as warrior, Niditch and Woods both comment on this metaphor; however, Dianne Bergant examines this analogy in the broader context of God-language. Bergant comments, "To ask, 'Is Yahweh a warrior?' is not unlike asking, 'Is God a father? Or a mother? Is God personal? Is God just?'"[15] Bergant affirms the theology that the metaphor is trying to express but rejects the images of God as warrior as "no longer apt expressions of such theology."[16]

In his seminal work on Old Testament theology, Walter Brueggemann explores further the metaphor of God as warrior. Brueggemann asserts that the metaphor is problematic because it "puts violence into the middle of Israel's speech about God, and it evidences that Israel celebrates God-sponsored, God-enacted violence."[17] He also states that "a theological interpretation of the Old Testament must face this problem which is intrinsic to Israel's God-talk."[18]

This next section looks at the warrior God motif as it appears in selected passages from the books of Isaiah and Zechariah. The ethical questions that remain in the foreground are, Is violence legitimate and if so, when? and, Is the picture of God as a commander-in-chief, a warrior, an accurate one, or is it an image that Israel projected onto God in an effort to make sense of its history as it attempted to offer people hope in the face of fear and the threat of defeat?

Isaiah 13:1–22

The book of Isaiah contains several prophecies against non-Israelite kingdoms and empires.[19] In 13:1–22, a prophecy against Babylon, the anticipated day of the Lord is to be one of judgment and pain for the Babylonians, enemies of Israel, and a nation of people who were emerging as a great superpower in the shadow of Assyria, an older superpower. This passage depicts God as a commander-in-chief who is "mustering an army for battle" (v. 4).

---

[13]Ibid., 155.

[14]See Woods, *Perspectives on War in the Bible*, 154–55.

[15]Dianne Bergant, "Yahweh: A Warrior God?" *The Bible Today* (May 1983): 160.

[16]Ibid., 163.

[17]Walter Brueggemann, *Theology of the Old Testament: Testimony, Dispute, Advocacy* (Minneapolis: Fortress Press, 1997), 243.

[18]Ibid. Brueggemann does a thorough analysis of the warrior God metaphor in pp. 241–47.

[19]See, e.g., Isaiah 13—23.

Following a brief superscription (v. 1), the passage opens with God's speaking through Isaiah, who is proclaiming to his audience the prophecy from God that he saw in a vision (vv. 2–3).[20] In verse 2, God issues a series of commands—"raise a signal," "cry aloud," "wave the hand"—to mobilize the armies for an attack on the nobles. Both the military personnel and the enemy are obscure. What is clear, however, is that God has commanded warriors:

> I myself have commanded by consecrated ones,
> have summoned my warriors, my proudly exulting ones,
> to execute my anger. (v. 3)

Verse 4 opens with a command for the audience to "listen." This command is repeated twice in the verse and sets the stage for the next series of events: the coming of an army—God's "weapons"—that represents God's indignation. This army comes from afar, is mustered by God for battle, and has as its mission the destruction of the whole earth (vv. 4–5).

Verses 6–10 describe the day of the Lord, which is near. This day will be a dreaded day, a "cruel" day, full of divine wrath and fierce anger, aimed at making the earth a desolation and destroying all sinners from it (v. 9). Verses 11–22 expand the vision of the day of the Lord to include what God plans to do personally through the Medes, whom God is stirring up against Babylon (v. 17). These verses describe the ravages of war, which include harm to those most vulnerable among the people—infants will be dashed to pieces (v. 16a), and women will be ravished (v. 16b). There will be no mercy on "the fruit of the womb" and no pity on the children (v. 18). Babylon will become "like Sodom and Gomorrah when God overthrew them" (v. 19). Brueggemann points out that "Babylon is not to be taken too literally but functions as a figure for any and every geopolitical power that runs against the intention of Yahweh."[21] Verses 20–22 describe further what Babylon will be like when God has finished with it. An empire no longer suited for human population, Babylon will become the resting place of wild animals and the home of howling creatures (vv. 21–22).

In summary, this poem is "an outraged, outrageous presentation of Yahweh's massive, brutal rule."[22] It presents to readers a picture of a merciless

---

[20]Brueggemann makes the claim that the speaker in verses 2–3 is unknown (see *Isaiah 1—39*, 116). Given these verses in the context of the entire poem, I argue that the speaker is God, who speaks through the prophet Isaiah; see also verses 11–22 in particular. The speaker in verses 4–10 is also God. In these verses, God refers to God's self in the third person, which is not atypical. See, e.g., Micah 2:12–13; 4:6–7; Isaiah 49:7.

[21]Ibid., 121.

[22]Ibid., 120.

God of power who, as commander-in-chief of a heartless and ruthless army, uses the power to command one group of people to devastate another. Festering divine anger and divine wrath is ready to erupt and will leave blistering effects on an empire and its people. Isaiah 13:1–22 confronts readers with the image of a God who ordains and sanctions a devastating military invasion. This Lord of hosts is Lord of heaven and earth (see vv. 10, 13) and reigns with terror. The text reflects the social and political situation of the ancient world and Israel's belief in a warrior God. Heard in a contemporary context, however, the text reminds readers of the devastating effects of war and violence and invites the human community to envision new metaphors for God that arise out of deep religious experiences in the ongoing struggle to become a people of peace in right relationship with God and all creation.

Isaiah 59:15b–20

The central issue in this poem is a lack of justice; the main theme is vengeance (vv. 15b, 17b). Here Isaiah sketches a verbal picture of a God who metaphorically resembles a warrior all decked out in military garb, donned for the purpose of bringing about justice in the midst of adversity (vv. 16–18). The work that warrior God will do is a work "which will display and satisfy his righteousness, save his people, repay his foes and be carried through to completion by the driving motivation of divine zeal"[23] (vv. 18–20).

From the text, one can glean a connection between justice, righteousness, salvation, and military intervention. Contemporary readers are left to ponder ways that justice, righteousness, and salvation might be accomplished without military intervention, so as to bring to fruition the eschatological vision of the prophet that celebrates a just God of peace:

> He shall judge between the nations,
> and shall arbitrate for many peoples;
> they shall beat their swords into plowshares,
> and their spears into pruning hooks;
> nation shall not lift up sword against nation,
> neither shall they learn war any more. (Isa. 2:4)

Zechariah 14:1–21

The warfare imagery of the day of the Lord continues in Zechariah 14:1–21. The passage opens with a foreboding superscription that leads

---

[23]J. Alec Motyer, *The Prophecy of Isaiah: An Introduction and Commentary* (Downers Grove, Ill.: InterVarsity Press, 1993), 491.

into the description of two battles, one in which God as commander-in-chief will gather all the nations against Jerusalem, and the other in which God will go forth and fight against those nations antagonistic toward Jerusalem (vv. 2, 3–5). The text highlights the horrors of war: a city captured, houses plundered, women raped, people exiled, with some remaining in the city (v. 2). Verses 6–11 speak of the transformation of the land, with the promise that "Jerusalem shall abide in security."

Verses 12–15 express the image of a punitive God who will do battle on behalf of Jerusalem. Note that the plagues promised to those who wage war against Jerusalem will affect not only the people but also the natural world. Such a threat of devastation by a plague harks back to Exodus 9:1—11:10 and 12:29–32, particularly to Exodus 9:1–7, which describes the affliction of the livestock by a deadly pestilence.

The final set of verses describes a celebration that is to occur in Jerusalem (vv. 14–21). The festival of booths will be commemorated, and Jerusalem and Judah will be dedicated completely to God once again.

This passage suggests to readers a variety of images, and it holds up as a model the image of God as a warrior. This image, found similarly in Isaiah 13:1–22 and 59:15b–20, inspires ongoing theological and hermeneutical reflection, especially in light of a global emphasis on and efforts toward world peace.

Gender-Specific Metaphorical Language and Imagery

A sense of violence can be communicated not only by impressions and perceptions of a God of punitive chastisement and a warrior God motif but also through gender-specific metaphorical language with related images. For example, in many passages throughout the books of the prophets, both the Northern Kingdom Israel and the Southern Kingdom Judah are accused of apostasy and idolatry. Oftentimes Israel and Judah, as well as Judah's capital Jerusalem, are referred to as a "harlot" and a "whore." In the prophetic texts, specifically in Hosea and Ezekiel, covenant relationship between God and the two kingdoms, with their respective people, is envisioned as a marital relationship with God as the husband and Israel and Judah as the wife.[24] This next part of the discussion focuses on selected texts from the prophets that contain gender-specific metaphors and that convey through the use of metaphorical language the suggestion of violence.

---

[24]A clear example of this expression can be found in Hosea 2:16–20.

Hosea 2:1–15

Hosea 2:1–15 is part of a larger unit, chapters 1—3, that focuses on the husband-wife metaphor. The setting for this passage is Hosea's bitter marital experience with Gomer, his promiscuous wife.[25] Like Gomer, Israel has been unfaithful to God, going after and worshiping Canaanite deities and thus breaking covenant.

Hosea 2:1–15 consists of three parts: verses 2–3, 4–5, and 6–15. In verse 1, Hosea issues a command to his two children, pleading with them to address their mother. Embedded in the prophet's words that follow is the metaphor of Israel as Gomer.

In verses 2–3, Hosea makes a passionate plea to his children to confront their mother about her adulterous ways, requesting that she stop such actions (v. 2). The punch line, however, comes in verse 3 where Hosea issues a threat. Either she stops her whoring or he will strip her naked, expose her, make her a wilderness, turn her into a parched land, and kill her with thirst (v. 3). On one level, these two verses apply to Gomer; on another level, they symbolically speak about God's relationship with Israel— Israel's infidelity and what God plans to do to Israel if "she" does not refrain from "her" whoring—"her" idolatrous ways.

Verses 4–5 continue the series of threats begun in verse 3. Hosea/ God states that "he" will have no pity on Gomer's/Israel's children because they are "children of whoredom" (v. 4). Verse 5 expands on verse 2. Hosea/ God describes in detail Gomer's/Israel's infidelities (v. 5).

Verses 6–15 state a series of punishments that husband Hosea/God will inflict on wife Gomer/Israel (vv. 6–13). Gomer/Israel stands accused of fickleness in infidelity and ignorance, for she did not know that it was her husband who had given her all sorts of gifts that were later used for Baal (vv. 6–8). Perhaps the most graphic and most brutal expression of punishment appears in verses 9–13 where Hosea/God declares that he will (1) take back his grain and wine, along with his wool and flax that was used to cover her nakedness; (2) uncover her shame in the sight of all her lovers; (3) allow no one to rescue her from his hand; (4) put an end to all her festivals; (5) lay waste her vines and her fig trees; and (6) punish her for her apostate ways and forgetfulness of him—Hosea/God.

Hosea/God then promises to lure Gomer/Israel into the wilderness after all these harsh punishments so that he can speak tenderly to her, give her vineyards, and thus win her back to himself, with her responding to him as she did in the days of her youth (vv. 14–15).

---

[25]For a concise and excellent comment on marriage and adultery in ancient Israel, see Gale A. Yee, "Hosea," in *Women's Bible Commentary,* expanded ed. with Apocrypha, ed. Carol A. Newsom and Sharon H. Ringe (Louisville, Ky.: Westminster John Knox Press, 1998), 209–10.

These verses depict Hosea/God as an enraged husband whose anger leads to several threats that are punitive and violent emotionally, physically, and psychologically for wife Gomer/Israel, who is to be mercilessly exposed to all her lovers. She will then be made to suffer serious consequences for her infidelity, only to be wooed again by her husband, whose anger has been expressed abusively.

This passage raises several ethical and theological points that Gale Yee highlights succinctly:

> Hosea's metaphor of the marriage between Yahweh and Israel gives an entrée into the human-divine relationship as no other metaphor can. It engages the reader in a compelling story about a God who is loving, forgiving, and compassionate, in spite of Israel's sinfulness. However, growing out of a social structure and value system that privileged male over female, this metaphor makes its theological point at the expense of real women and children who were and still are victims of sexual violence. When the metaphorical character of the biblical image is forgotten, a husband's physical abuse of his wife comes to be as justified as God's retribution against Israel.[26]

Given these insights, contemporary believers and readers are faced with a series of problems generated first by the initial understanding of covenant as a marital relationship, and second by the gender-specific metaphorical language that brings the marital notion of covenant to life. The questions become, then, How humanly and divinely ethical is Hosea's message, which speaks of violence being used as a corrective for violence? and, How appropriate is this metaphor for today when speaking about covenant and relationships? To such questions, Yee adds a further comment:

> The male violence embedded in the text of Hosea as it stands should make readers, both male and female, wary of an uncritical acceptance of its marriage metaphor. Moreover, the imaging of God as male/husband becomes difficult when one forgets the metaphor God is *like* a husband and insists literally that God *is* a husband and therefore always male.[27]

---

[26]Ibid., 212.

[27]Ibid. For further discussion on Hosea 2:1–15 and the implications of gender-specific metaphorical language, see Alice A. Keefe, "The Female Body, the Body Politic and the Land: A Sociopolitical Reading of Hosea 1—2," in *A Feminist Companion to the Latter Prophets,* ed. Athalya Brenner, FCB 8 (Sheffield, England: Sheffield Academic Press, 1995), 70–100; Naomi Graetz, "God Is to Israel as Husband Is to Wife: The Metaphoric Battering of Hosea's Wife," ibid., 126–45.

In conclusion, the metaphorical language in Hosea 2:1–15 calls for a reappropriation of the prophet's message in light of contemporary life experiences that reflect situations of violence and abuse, inclusive of marital infidelities and discords that have ended violently. And while the language of the passage may reflect the social setting and cultural perspectives of its day, such language has the potential to negatively affect one's theological imagination as well as one's understanding of and relationship with God and with other human beings. Thus, Hosea 2:1–15 inspires further ethical and hermeneutical reflection and invites the creation of new metaphors that call people to an abiding sense of respect and integrity in all relationships even in the face of human frailty and infidelity.

Ezekiel 23:1–49

Graphic in its descriptions and pointed in its accusations, the story about two sisters in Ezekiel 23:1–49 advances the theme of gender-specific metaphorical language as it recounts the tale of God's relationship with these two women of whoredom. The first woman, Oholah, symbolizes Samaria; the second, Oholibah, is Jerusalem. The passage opens with Ezekiel's proclaiming "the word of the Lord" that had come to him (v. 1). The actual story begins in verse 2. Here, God addresses Ezekiel directly and provides him with background information pertaining to the two sisters (vv. 2–4). Both are women of the same mother; both played the whore in Egypt and in their youth; both were caressed and fondled; both became God's and bore sons and daughters.

Following an initial description of the general situation and the sisters' whorings, God next describes Oholah's whorings and the divine punishment bestowed upon her for such conduct (vv. 5–10). Verses 9–10 admit a horrible scene of violence. Because Oholah betrayed God, God handed "her" over to her lovers, "into the hands of the Assyrians," who uncovered her nakedness, seized her sons and daughters, and killed her. God concludes with the comment, "Judgment was executed upon her, and she became a byword among women" (v. 10). These verses suggest an image of God as someone who deals violently with those guilty of infidelity. Here, the execution of justice for adultery is death. For male readers, the text, as it stands, condones capital punishment for breach of covenant relationship on the part of the woman.

Following the comments about Oholah, God describes Oholah's sister, Oholibah, who is said to be even more corrupt than her sister (vv. 11–21). Not only did she lust after many Assyrians, she also lusted after stately Chaldean figures carved on the wall and sent messengers to them in Chaldea, which resulted in the Babylonians' coming to her and lying with her. Thus, she had relations with both the Assyrians and Babylonians, Israel's two principal enemies (vv. 12–17). God's response to her was rejection (v. 18).

Disgusted with her whorings, God plans to take severe action against Oholibah (vv. 22–35). God pledges to bring her lovers against her (vv. 22–24); they will physically wound her (v. 25), harm her sons and daughters and destroy her survivors with fire (v. 25), strip her of her clothes and fine jewels (v. 26), and turn her over to those whom she hates, who will strip her, leaving her bare, with the nakedness of her whorings exposed (vv. 28–29). Furthermore, God pledges to give Oholibah the cup of suffering that was given to her sister, Oholah, and she must drink from it (vv. 31–34). Finally, in a cold and judgmental tone, God condemns Oholibah:

> Because you have forgotten me and cast me behind your back, therefore bear the consequences of your lewdness and whorings. (v. 35)

In summary, verses 22–35 portray God as someone who will not tolerate infidelity and idolatry. This God will mete out severe punishment directly and through others.

The picture shifts in verses 36–49. These verses are a dialogue between God and Ezekiel. In verses 36–42, God addresses the prophet; in verses 43–45 the prophet responds; and in verses 46–49, God offers a final response. In verses 36–42 and 43–45, both God and Ezekiel comment on the transgressions—the adulterous and idolatrous ways—of Oholah and Oholibah. The narrative closes with God's calling for the death of the two women through stoning. Also to be killed are their sons and daughters (v. 47). The entire story closes with one last assertive and judgmental word from God to the two sisters:

> They shall repay you for your lewdness, and you shall bear the penalty for your sinful idolatry; and you shall know that I am the Lord GOD. (v. 49)

The final phrase is an assertion of both God's sovereignty and God's power. Here, both are associated with the enactment and sanction of violent deeds that are meant to counter violence and transgression.

In summary, Ezekiel 23:1–49 is a literary narrative that describes a historical and religious reality, namely the transgression of covenant—the violation of right relationship between God and the people of Israel and Judah—embodied in the references to the kingdoms' capital cities of Samaria and Jerusalem and symbolized by two sisters, Oholah (Samaria) and Oholibah (Jerusalem).[28] The text depicts God as a scorned, forgotten lover and husband who, enraged, punishes his adulterous wife to the point of death. Justice is strict and without compassion. As a whole, the texts reflect the demise of both the Northern and Southern Kingdoms, along with their capital cities.

Heard in a contemporary setting, Ezekiel 23:1–49 relates a distressing message, and readers are left to ponder the ethical implications and ramifications of the prophet's words. Katheryn Pfisterer Darr remarks that

> the violence inflicted on these two "women" raises disturbing questions. Should one simply accept the enraged husband's explanation of why his wives deserved to be murdered? For Ezekiel, the enormity of Jerusalem's destruction required that the people's sins be depicted as proportionately heinous, lest the justice of God be doubted. Nevertheless, his use of female imagery is problematic, for he depicts female sexuality as the object of male possession and control, presents physical abuse as a way to reclaim such control, and then suggests that violence can be a means toward *healing* a broken relationship.[29]

Thus, gender-specific language and metaphors, coupled with an expression of divine justice that is accomplished through violence, has the potential of adding to the already devastating web of violence. Moreover, this text as a prophetic proclamation meant to highlight injustices while calling people to covenant loyalty, Torah, justice, and right relationships, presents an ethical vision in dire need of transformation. Other prophetic texts subvert Ezekiel's vision and assert that the way to the restoration of broken relationships is not through punitive chastisements or expressions of violence; rather, it is through acts of justice tempered by compassion that demonstrate concerted efforts at reconciliation, as the prophet Hosea suggests in 11:8–9 and 14:4–7.

Nahum 3:1–7

Another text that features the use of gender-specific metaphorical language is Nahum 3:1–7. Addressed to the city of Nineveh, this prophecy links the city's injustices to idolatry. Nineveh, depicted as a female, is destined to suffer the consequences of her actions, for God is "against" the city and will punish it by "lifting up" its skirts to "expose" its nakedness, and by

---

[28]It is not uncommon in the ancient Near Eastern world and in the Hebrew text to depict cities as feminine/females.

[29]Katheryn Pfisterer Darr, "Ezekiel," in *Women's Bible Commentary*, 198.

throwing filth at it, treating it with contempt, and by making it "a spectacle" (vv. 5–6).

In summary, the ethical message conveyed by both prophet and text is one in need of hermeneutical comment and creative re-visioning if the prophetic word is to be a source of hope for all.[30]

The Justice of a "Just" God in Context

Selected texts from the prophets that focus on God as a God of punitive justice, a warrior God, and a husband forgotten and forsaken all convey an ethical message that reflects the religious, social, historical, and cultural thought and realities of the day. In each of these three areas, justice is achieved through an assertion of power that causes pain, suffering, and even death to others. While metaphorical language raises the text to the level of symbolism, the metaphors used are either inherently violent or provide opportunities for the expression of violence. That justice be done as a response to injustice is an ethical responsibility to which the prophets call all people. But that justice be accomplished through violence is a situation that calls for further ethical reflection in light of Isaiah 2:1–4 and 65:17–25, which speak of an end to violence as new heavens and a new earth are ushered in.

---

[30]For further study on other texts of the Prophets and their relation to gender-specific metaphorical language, their links to violence, and their ethical implications, see Dempsey, *The Prophets,* 36–41, 64–67, and 95–103.

CHAPTER 6

Re-visioning Worship

The Prophets' Ethical Challenge

Since the beginning of creation, celebration has been part of the divine plan, with the seventh day—the Sabbath—being God's gift to the newly created world that was enjoyed by human and nonhuman life.[1] Indeed, the whole of Genesis 1—2 speaks of a "liturgy of creation," for

> it proclaims that the world God brings into being is an *orderly world*, created and shaped by God's purposive design, a *ritual world* in which the liturgy of creation might be sustained (Gen. 1:1—2:4a), and a *relational world* in which God invites humankind to share responsibility for the maintenance, development, and restoration of God's purposive designs for the universe (Gen. 2:4b–25).[2]

Hence, "the liturgy of creation…is the summons to celebrate and participate in the ordered, ritual, and relational world that God calls into existence."[3]

Within the Pentateuch, one of the earliest expressions of celebration is found in Genesis 8:20–22, where Noah builds an altar to God and gives burnt offerings on the occasion of the flood's end. Samuel E. Balentine sees this as the first *act* of worship,[4] and as a result of Noah's deed, God

---

[1]See Horst Dietrich Preuss, *Old Testament Theology,* vol. 2, OTL (Louisville, Ky.: Westminster John Knox Press, 1996), 235. See also Genesis 2:1–3 and Exodus 20:8–11. The sabbatical year embraced the spirit of the sabbath day; see, e.g., Exodus 23:10–13; Leviticus 25:1–7; and Deuteronomy 15:1–18.

[2]Samuel E. Balentine, *The Torah's Vision of Worship,* OBT (Minneapolis: Fortress Press, 1999), 81.

[3]Ibid.

[4]Ibid., 115.

makes a promise never again to curse the ground because of humankind (Gen. 8:21). A divine covenant that God makes with all creation follows the divine promise (Gen. 9:1–17). The theme of covenant and worship continues in Genesis 15—17, which Balentine identifies as the first *words* of worship.[5] Thus, there is a relationship between creation, covenant, and worship that is made manifest through the Israelites' participation in festival and sacrifice.

As a community, the Israelites were a people of celebration, and many of their festivals were associated with the seasons. For example, the harvest festival, otherwise known as the Festival of Weeks, occurred at the beginning of the harvest of wheat (Ex. 23:16; 34:22; Deut. 16:9f.). The Autumn festival, also known as Tabernacles, began originally as a festival to conclude the harvest of grapes, figs, and olives (Deut. 16:13). Later, this festival was expanded to include a ritual of atonement and a remembrance of salvation history (Lev. 16; 23:42f.; Num. 29:12–38). The festival of Mazzoth, originally separate from Passover, commemorated the beginning of the barley harvest. Other festivals included Passover, New Year's, Purim, and Hanukkah, to name a few. Lastly, within the Old Testament, there are "festival calendars" that can be found in the Covenant Code (Ex. 23:14–17), the Law of YHWH's Privilege (Ex. 34:18–24), Deuteronomy (Deut. 16:1–17), the Holiness Code (Lev. 23:4–44), and in Numbers 28—29.[6] One other event that the Israelites celebrated was circumcision, an act associated with covenant that began with Abraham (Gen. 17:9–27; 21:4). As the tradition developed, emphasis was placed on the symbolic circumcision of the foreskin of one's heart (Deut. 10:16; Jer. 4:4). Covenant, then, implied a way of life that would go beyond an external physical sign.

Sacrifices were also a part of Israel's worship. Various types of sacrifices included: burnt offerings (Lev. 1:1–17), cereal offerings (Lev. 2:1–16), well-being offerings (Lev. 3:1–17), purification offerings (Lev. 4:1–35), and reparation offerings (Lev. 5:14–26), among others.[7] One particular sacrifice that was strongly condemned in Israel was the sacrifice of children. This practice was associated with the term "Molech,"[8] and the biblical text indicates that the Israelites did participate in such sacrifices.[9] Despite this

---

[5]Ibid.

[6]For a detailed discussion of Israel's festivals, see Preuss, *Old Testament Theology*, 2:224–35.

[7]For a full discussion of some of Israel's sacrifices, see Jacob Milgrom, *Leviticus 1–16*, AB 3 (New York: Doubleday, 1991), 133–489, and Preuss, *Old Testament Theology*, vol. 2, 238–45.

[8]See, e.g., Leviticus 20:5f.; Deuteronomy 18:10; 2 Kings 17:17; and 2 Chronicles 33:6.

[9]See Judges 8:21; 11:31ff.; and 1 Kings 16:33–34.

horrifying dimension of sacrifice, this aspect of Israel's life as a worshiping community was intricately connected to the people's understanding of God as the one who saves.

In the context of Israel's history, Bruce Birch, Walter Brueggemann, Terence Fretheim, and David Petersen assert that sacrifices "are tangible means through which God acts in a saving way on behalf of the faithful worshiper; sacrifices are sacramentally conceived."[10] Furthermore, the biblical text suggests that for the Israelite people, sacrificial offerings, along with the confession of their sins, were one way that they could seek divine pardon and renew their relationship with their God.[11] Finally, worship is linked to the work of creation; it is "a God-given way for the people of God to participate in the re-creation of a new world."[12] This point becomes clear in the writings of the prophets, which not only mention the festivals[13] but also make a connection between worship and ethical practice that has as its goal the restoration of right relationships and the re-creation of a new world. This chapter focuses on the relationship between worship and ethical practice as seen in the prophets and the implications that the prophetic message has for readers today.

Many texts within the Pentateuch highlight Israel's festivals, rituals, and sacrificial offerings. All these expressions helped to establish Israel as a community in relationship with its God, faithful to Torah, which called for the people's single-hearted devotion. In the writings of the prophets, however, one hears of God's repeated rejection of Israel's sacrificial offerings and expressions of worship when ritual becomes disconnected from right relationships. Various texts within the books of Isaiah, Jeremiah, and Amos depict God's refusing to accept the people's offerings and reprimanding them severely for their infidelity to Torah.

Isaiah 1:10–17 and 29:13–14

Divine condemnation of Israel's sacrifices and expressions of worship is heard in Isaiah 1:10–17 and 29:13–14. In 1:10–17, Isaiah delivers God's stinging word to his listeners. The passage begins on a metaphorical note that addresses the Judahites and its rulers and people, comparing them to the "rulers of Sodom" and the "people of Gomorrah" (v. 10).[14] The allusion

---

[10]Birch, Brueggemann, Fretheim, and Petersen, *A Theological Introduction to the Old Testament*, 159.

[11]Ibid. See also Leviticus 5:5–6; Numbers 5:7; and 1 Samuel 7:6.

[12]Ibid.

[13]See, e.g., Isaiah 1:14; 30:29; Amos 4:4f.; 5:21; Ezekiel 45:21–25, and so forth.

[14]See Genesis 19:1–29.

to Sodom and Gomorrah, two cities rejected by God, and the Judahites' being identified with them not only highlights Judah's depravity but also indicates God's disdain for Judah. Verse 11 features God boldly rejecting the people's sacrifices:

> What to me is the multitude of your sacrifices?
> says the LORD;
> I have had enough of burnt offerings of rams
> and the fat of fed beasts;
> I do not delight in the blood of bulls,
> or of lambs, or of goats.

Verses 12–15 continue the same sentiments, with God's requesting that the people cease trampling the divine courts, for their offerings are "futile" and their incense an "abomination" (v. 13a). In verses 13b–14, God expresses intense disgust at the ritual celebrations:

> New moon and sabbath and calling of convocation—
> I cannot endure solemn assemblies
> with iniquity.
> Your new moons and your appointed festivals
> my soul hates;
> They have become a burden to me,
> I am weary of bearing them.

The main point expressed here is that neither sacrifices nor rituals are met with divine favor because those offering the sacrifices and celebrating the rituals are an iniquitous people (v. 13b). The formal divine response comes in verses 15–17. In verse 15, God makes it clear to the people engaged in various expressions of worship that there will be no divine response. God will hide God's eyes from them and will not listen to them because their hands are "full of blood." The people's gestures of worship are rejected because they are "no longer vehicles for a serious relationship. The offerings are dishonest."[15]

Finally, in verses 16–17, God gives a divine injunction, requesting the people to wash themselves, make themselves clean, remove their evil doings from God's eyes, cease doing evil, embrace the good, seek justice, rescue the oppressed, defend the orphan, and plead for the widow. These nine

---

[15]Walter Brueggemann, *Isaiah 1—39,* WestBC (Louisville: Westminster John Knox Press, 1998), 17.

imperatives have as their goal the restoration of right relationship with their God, whom they have forsaken (see Isa. 1:4). Thus, Isaiah's message suggests that a connection exists between "right worship (holiness)" and "right neighbor practice (justice),"[16] a theme to be explored further in the next major section of this chapter.

Mention of insincere worship occurs in Isaiah 29:13–14. In a traditional judgment speech, God through the prophet condemns those people among the Judahite community who give their pious words to God but not their hearts, and who worship God because it is the thing to do according to the Law. In sum, both Isaiah 1:10–17 and 29:13–14 suggest to readers that sacrifice and pious practices are meaningless if they do not flow from and contribute to right relationship with one's God and with one another.

Jeremiah 6:16–21 and 7:21–26

In Jeremiah 6:16–21, the prophet delivers a divine judgment speech to his listeners in which he makes known to them God's displeasure with their sacrifices. In essence, holy deeds are no substitute for a life of justice and righteousness. The passage opens with God's addressing the Judahites through Jeremiah (vv. 16–17). God offers them words of instruction and encouragement, which, according to God's rendition of their response, they have rejected. Verse 18 introduces the first statement of impending divine chastisement, which comes to the fore in verses 19–20.

In verse 19, God calls on the earth to act as a witness and then makes the announcement that disaster, divinely ordained, is about to befall the people because they have paid no heed to God's words and have rejected God's teaching. In verse 20, God declares their offerings and sacrifices unacceptable:

> Of what use to me is frankincense that comes from Sheba,
> or sweet cane from a distant land?
> Your burnt offerings are not acceptable,
> nor are your sacrifices pleasing to me.

Frankincense was one of the main ingredients used in incense offered to God, and the fact that it came from a distance—Sheba—along with the sweet cane from a distant land points out that great effort was made to acquire those products that were part of a ritual offering to God. The burnt offerings involved the sacrifice of an animal. Burnt offerings held a prominent place in the community because they were often offered daily or on a continual basis.

---

[16]Ibid., 19.

Together, verses 19–20 depict what seems to be Jeremiah's rejection of Israel's sacrificial system. William Holladay, however, points out that "the prophets, including Jrm, did not so much have in mind a cultless religion as they were insistent that personal and communal responsiveness takes priority, and that any cultic act unaccompanied by loyalty and sensitivity was meaningless."[17]

The passage closes with a second statement of impending divine chastisement (v. 21). This text makes clear that any type of offering or sacrifice is pointless unless it is accompanied by a proper attitude that leads to the embracing and living out of God's words and ways, a theme picked up in Jeremiah 7:21–26.

In 7:21–26, God speaks through Jeremiah and makes clear that what is required of the people is not burnt offerings and sacrifices, but obedience to God and God's ways so that life may go well for them. And, as the text indicates, this is where the problem lies. The people have not listened to God; they have gone their own way, and this has led to vice instead of virtue (v. 24). Hence, Jeremiah's message here, as well as in 6:16–21, suggests that there is a link between what one offers to God and how one lives one's life in relation to God and God's ways.

Amos 4:4–5 and 5:21–24

One of the strongest condemnations of the official cult as sinful occurs in Amos 4:4–5. With tongue in cheek, God, speaking through Amos, challenges the Israelites to transgress and even to multiply transgression while they simultaneously engage in ritual activities:

> Come to Bethel—and transgress;
> to Gilgal—and multiply transgression;
> bring your sacrifices every morning,
> your tithes every three days;
> bring a thank-offering of leavened bread,
> and proclaim freewill offerings, publish them. (vv. 4–5a)

Verse 5b closes the unit and captures the entire sentiment of divine condemnation as communicated by the passage, "For so you love to do, O people of Israel!" Thus, Amos exposes the disparity between the people's worship and their way of living.

In Amos 5:21–24, divine dissatisfaction with the Israelites' rituals is expressed again. Here, God states boldly, "I hate, I despise your festivals, and I take no delight in your solemn assemblies" (v. 21). Moreover, God rejects the people's burnt offerings, grain offerings, and well-being offerings

---

[17]Holladay, *Jeremiah 1*, 223.

(v. 22). After requesting that all song and music be silenced (v. 23), God calls for justice to "roll down like waters, and righteousness like an ever-flowing stream" (v. 24). Without a doubt, Amos makes the point that God couldn't care less about the people's offerings and sacrifices, especially when they are being made by a people sunk in the mire of transgression. What God desires is justice and righteousness, hence, right relationships that embrace the spirit of Torah with its vision for love and its call to an ethical way of life.[18]

The divine call for justice and righteousness in Amos 5:21–24 creates the backdrop for the next group of texts from Hosea, Isaiah, and Micah, which focus on the kind of sacrifice most desirable to God.

Hosea 6:4–6

Addressed to both Israel and Judah, this passage opens with God's directing to the two kingdoms two rhetorical questions that express divine frustration and bewilderment (v. 4a). Then, with metaphorical language, God declares to them the instability and unreliability of their love (v. 4b), which, according to covenant, should be loyal and steadfast. Seeing their condition, God next recounts what has been done on their behalf, namely the exercise of punitive divine justice.[19] The passage reaches its climax in verse 6 as God makes known the kind of worship that is desirable:

> For I desire steadfast love and not sacrifice,
> the knowledge of God rather than burnt offerings.

Hearing this verse both in the context of Hosea's time, specifically, the eighth century B.C.E., and in the context of relationship and covenant, Bruce Birch comments:

> It is the committed love of covenant partnership with God and the knowledge that comes from experienced relationship with God that truly make a difference…Such love and knowledge of God have been made available to Israel and Judah in ongoing relationship to the God revealed in the Exodus, in the wilderness wandering, and in giving of the covenant and law. But the people have focused on the religious rituals and practices rather than on relationship to the God those practices were intended to honor.[20]

---

[18]See, e.g., Deuteronomy 6:1–9 and 10:12–22. For additional comment on worship and cult, see Hosea 8:11–14; 9:4–6; Malachi 1:6–14; 2:10–14; Joel 1:1–13, among others.

[19]Hans Walter Wolff points out that "the perfect verbs and the plural noun suggest that the verse refers to the earlier prophets in the Northern Kingdom, such as Ahijah of Shilo, Elijah, Micaiah ben Imlah, and Amos, as well as Hosea's own proclamation (5:8f, 14)." See *Hosea,* 120.

[20]Birch, *Hosea, Joel, and Amos,* 69.

Thus, true worship is not defined solely by ritual practice; rather, it consists of an attitude and way of life characterized by justice, righteousness, and steadfast love—the hallmarks of covenant and the necessary ingredients for right relationships with all creation (compare Jer. 9:24).

Isaiah 58:6–14

Following a statement on false worship (vv. 1–5) is one on true worship (vv. 6–14), where Isaiah outlines the kind of fast that God desires. This fast involves neither animal nor grain sacrifice offered as a sign of atonement. Rather, it is to be a fast of *mishpat, sedeqa,* and *hesed*—a fast of justice, righteousness, and loving-kindness—expressed through acts of liberation, care, comfort, integrity, and respect. It is to be a fast that has as its goal the renewal and restoration of right relationships.

As a polemic "directed against a group described as self-righteous and meticulous in religious observances,"[21] the passage calls for the loosening of the bonds of injustice, the undoing of the thongs of the yoke, the setting free of the oppressed, the breaking of every yoke (v. 6), the sharing of one's bread with the hungry, the sheltering of the homeless, the clothing of the naked, the offering of hospitality to one's kin (v. 7), the cessation of judgmental actions and malicious speech (v. 9), and the honoring of the Sabbath. (v. 13) Thus, what God did for the Israelites during the time of the Exodus, they are now encouraged to do for one another. By doing so, they would be fulfilling Torah, which calls them to embody and live out a life of love (see Deut. 6:1–8; 7:7–11; 10:12–22). Paul Hanson comments:

> In a community where those who regarded themselves as the most religious had converted religion into private acts of study and ritual, thereby leaving the entire realm of social relations and commerce under the dominion of ruthless, self-serving exploitation, the prophet reaffirms the classical understanding of Yahwism that grew out of the experience of God's liberating slaves from their bondage, feeding them in the wilderness, and giving them a homeland of their own. It is a rigorously moral understanding that places the one who would be true to God on the side of the same ones whom God reached out to help and empower, those suffering injustice at the hands of authorities, those imprisoned for acts of conscience, those denied housing and proper clothing, those turned away even by their own relatives. The appeal is an impassioned one to the heart of the community.

---

[21]Paul D. Hanson, *Isaiah 40—66,* Interpretation (Louisville, Ky.: Westminster John Knox Press, 1995), 204.

It is a plea to reclaim authentic humanity by replacing cold, calculating self-interest with acts of loving-kindness that restore genuine communal solidarity.[22]

The community's responsiveness to one another has a direct effect on how God will respond to the community. Isaiah instructs his listeners that when they live out a life of love in accordance with Torah, God will answer them when they call (v. 9). God will guide them continually, satisfy their needs in parched places, make their bones strong (v. 11), enable them to ride upon the heights of the earth (v. 14a), and feed them with the heritage of their ancestor Jacob (v. 14b). As the people care for one another, so their God will care for them. Furthermore, their light shall break forth like the dawn (v. 8a; compare v. 10b); they will be healed and protected by God (v. 8); and they will be like a watered garden whose waters flow continuously (v. 11). Their ancient ruins shall be rebuilt, and they themselves shall raise up the foundations of many generations and be called "the repairer of the breach" and "the restorer of streets to live in" (v. 12); they shall take delight in their Lord (v. 14).

In summary, Isaiah heralds a vision of worship that must exceed faithfulness to external practices and rituals. Isaiah redefines worship as the lived experience of being in right relationship with one another and with God, made manifest through ethical practice rooted in and flowing from divine love (see Deut. 6:1–8), which demands justice, righteousness, and compassion.

Micah 6:6–8

Isaiah's vision of worship is also found in the book of Micah, specifically in 6:6–8. With heartfelt words, the prophet muses out loud to God on behalf of his sinful community, for whom he is interceding:

> With what shall I come before the LORD,
> and bow myself before God on high?
> Shall I come before him with burnt offerings,
> with calves a year old?
> Will the LORD be pleased with thousands of rams,
> with then thousands of rivers of oil?
> Shall I give my firstborn for my transgression,
> the fruit of my body for the sin of my soul? (vv. 6–7)

The response to Micah's four questions comes in the form of a statement that concludes with a question:

---

[22]Ibid., 205–6.

He has told you, O mortal, what is good;
and what does the LORD require of you
but to do justice, and to love kindness,
and to walk humbly with your God? (v. 8)[23]

In this verse, justice implies a social responsibility. "To do justice means to work for the establishment of equity for all, especially for the powerless."[24] The phrase "to love kindness" implies loyalty and covenant relationship: loyalty to God, God's loyalty to the people, and the people's loyalty to one another. Finally, "to walk humbly with your God" describes the whole orientation of Israel's life. First, it is a call to live in a simple and dynamic relationship with God, and second, it is a call to walk in God's ways. James Limburg notes that "in Judaism the word for ethics is *halacha* which means 'walking'; the idea is that the task of ethics is to describe how one ought to walk one's day-by-day life."[25]

In summary, Micah's words reflect his community's notion of worship (vv. 6–7), and instruct and call the community to a deeper understanding and expression of worship (v. 8) that has been elucidated by Isaiah in Isaiah 58:6–14. With respect to Micah's community, Leslie Allen asks, "If *hesed* modeled upon their Lord's is cherished among them, then will the covenant purpose of God have reached its goal in the establishment of a society where theology and ethics are one?"[26] For believing communities today, Micah 6:6–8 offers a challenging and disturbing message. Pious acts of reparation offered to God are not what God desires; rather, God requires that one be in right relationship, which is the only true avenue to reconciliation that leads to enduring peace.

The Prophets' Vision of Worship in Context

Various texts within the Old Testament, and specifically within the Pentateuch, shed light on the kinds of sacrifices, rituals, and festivals that composed Israel's understanding of worship and the importance of it in the life of the community. Selected texts within the writings of the prophets indicate a move on the part of some prophets to declare that love of God

---

[23]On the point of human sacrifice, James Limburg points out that "the old story about Abraham and Isaac (Gen. 22) had made clear that the Lord did not want human sacrifices. While Israel's neighbors continued the practice (2 Kings 3:27), and while it even took place in Judah in certain extreme situations (2 Kings 16:3; 21:6), human sacrifice was never allowed in Israelite religion, and the prophets spoke sharply against it (Jer. 19:5; Ezek. 16:20; see also Deut. 12:31; 18:10)." See *Hosea-Micah*, Interpretation (Atlanta: John Knox Press, 1988), 191.

[24]Limburg, *Hosea-Micah*, 192. See also Leslie C. Allen, *The Books of Joel, Obadiah, Jonah, and Micah*, NICOT (Grand Rapids, Mich.: Eerdmans, 1976).

[25]Ibid., 193.

[26]Allen, *The Books of Joel, Obadiah, Jonah, and Micah*, 374.

and love of neighbor are no longer to be seen as mutually exclusive of each other, but that, in fact, they are related and interdependent. Hence, worship implies faithfulness to covenant and Torah as a way of life that governs one's relationship with God and God's people.

Furthermore, the prophets' message about worship and praxis suggests to readers that right relationship with God and with one another is integral to the renewal, restoration, and transformation of the human community, and that when worship is redefined and understood as inseparable from a life of justice, righteousness, and compassion, worship then becomes "a God-given way for the people of God to participate in the re-creation of a new world."[27] Today, this participation in the re-creation of a new world demands that the people of God act with justice, righteousness, and compassion toward nonhuman life as well if the re-creation of a new world is to be just that—the re-creation of a new world. God's justice, righteousness, and compassion is for all creation (see Ps. 104:1–30; compare Wis. 11:12–26; and Sir. 18:13), and all creation is invited to join in the dance of life and the litany of praise (see Ps. 19:1–4 and 148).

---

[27]Birch, Brueggemann, Fretheim, and Petersen, *A Theological Introduction to the Old Testament,* 159.

CHAPTER 7

Cosmic Redemption

Embracing the Prophetic Vision and Spirit

The ancient prophet Joel once delivered the following vision to a people waiting for a word of hope:

> Then afterward
> I will pour out my spirit on all flesh;
> your sons and your daughters shall prophesy,
> your old men shall dream dreams,
> and your young men shall see visions.
> Even on the male and female slaves,
> in those days, I will pour out my spirit. (Joel 2:28–29)

Joel's vision continues to be a word of hope for those reading and hearing this text in the third millennium and twenty-first century, a time full of grace, grandeur, and promise, but not without challenges and struggles that, in some instances, far surpass those of the early Israelites.

Sadly, the dawn of the third millennium and the twenty-first century has not seen the end of oppression and injustice, and both have increased to the extent that the entire planet with all its life forms now suffers pain and devastation. Consequently, all creation gropes for a vision of wholeness, a word of hope, a message of comfort.

This experience of suffering that affects the entire community of life was noted by theologian Elizabeth A. Johnson in the 1993 Madeleva Lecture in Spirituality titled "Women, Earth, and Creator Spirit." In this lecture, she quoted Brian Patrick, who re-visions the concepts of neighbor and community: "Who is our neighbor: the Samaritan? the outcast? the enemy? Yes, yes, of course. But it is also the whale, the dolphin, and the rain forest. Our neighbor is the entire community of life, the entire universe. We must love it all as our self."[1] Johnson then linked this broader sense of community to the prophetic tradition and called for a new ethic:

> A flourishing humanity on a thriving earth: such is the vision that shapes the prophetic course. Since it is the earth that is being destabilized by human practice, redressing the balance requires increased focus on the integrity of natural systems and the worth of non-human creatures. Accordingly, prophecy converted to the earth sees that making a preferential option for the poor includes other species and the ravaged natural world itself. Healing and redeeming this world, this intrinsically valuable matrix of our origin, growth, and fulfillment, has the character of a moral imperative. It urges us to act according to the criterion crafted by the naturalist Aldo Leopold: "A thing is right when it tends to preserve the integrity, stability, and beauty of the life community. It is wrong when it tends to do otherwise." We are as large as our loves. The prophetic option for a biocentric ethic transforms us toward great-heartedness in its demand for universal compassion and cosmic praxis.[2]

Reflecting on the words of Joel and hearing them in the context of the Christian tradition (see Acts 2:14–18) and ongoing theological reflection, one can see that God's spirit has been poured out on all flesh, and God's people are prophesying. What is new is the call for a biocentric ethic. And given a new understanding of community, one can no longer talk about "social justice" and "social ethics." What is needed is a socioecological vision of justice and an ethic that embraces all creation and works toward its liberation and redemption. The seeds for such a holistic ethic can be unearthed in the vision of Israel's prophets. When reread and heard in a contemporary cosmological context, the prophets' message grounds the new ethic in the ever-ancient, ever-new prophetic tradition, whose eschatological vision of new heavens and a new earth has already begun to unfold.

---

[1] Elizabeth A. Johnson, *Women, Earth, and Creator Spirit* (Mahwah, N.J.: Paulist Press, 1993), 67. See also Michael Dowd, *Earthspirit: A Handbook for Nurturing an Ecological Christianity* (Mystic, Conn.: Twenty-Third Publications, 1991), 40, where Brian Patrick's comment is quoted.

[2] Ibid.; see also Aldo Leopold, *A Sand County Almanac* (New York: Oxford University Press, 1949), 224–25.

Embracing the Prophetic Vision

In "Hope Amidst Crisis: A Prophetic Vision of Cosmic Redemption,"[3] I argue rigorously the following three points:

1. The redemption of humankind is linked to the natural world, and the natural world's experience of transformation and new creation often happens in the process of humanity's being redeemed from its sinfulness, liberated from its oppressive situations, and healed of the sufferings it undergoes on account of its sinfulness.

2. The natural world can provide delightful and invigorating images, metaphors, and similes that allow people to envision how beautiful and liberating life can be when there is a sense of balance, order, reverence for, and relationship with all of creation.

3. God's plan for salvation is one of cosmic redemption secured by promises that are divine and eschatological.[4]

Various texts within the books of the Prophets support this argument and provide a vision of cosmic redemption for all creation.[5]

Selected passages from Isaiah and Ezekiel suggest that the redemption of humankind from sin and suffering is connected to the celebration and restoration of the natural world. In Isaiah 44:23 the natural world is invited to rejoice because the Israelites have been redeemed:

Sing, O heavens, for the LORD has done it;
shout, O depths of the earth;
break forth into singing, O mountains,
O forest, and every tree in it!
For the LORD has redeemed Jacob,
and will be glorified in Israel.

The natural world is invited to sing a second time in Isaiah 49:13. Its song is a response to God's comfort and compassion extended to those who suffer.

Ezekiel 36:33–36 suggests that a relationship exists between the redemption of humanity from sin and the restoration of the land. The passage opens with Ezekiel's delivering God's word whereby God promises to cleanse the people of their iniquities (v. 33a). This is followed by God's promise to cause the towns to be inhabited and the waste places rebuilt

---

[3]Carol J. Dempsey, in *All Creation Is Groaning: An Interdisciplinary Vision for Life in a Sacred Universe,* ed. Carol J. Dempsey and Russell A. Butkus (Collegeville, Minn.: Liturgical Press, 1999), 269–84.

[4]Ibid., 276.

[5]For a full discussion of this argument and related texts, see ibid.

(v. 33b). Finally, not until after the people are cleansed of their iniquities does the desolate land become "like the garden of Eden" (v. 35a) and the desolate and ruined towns become inhabited and fortified once again (v. 35b).

Isaiah, Hosea, and Amos speak of the renewal of covenant and the vision of harmonious relationships. In Isaiah 2:1–4 the prophet envisions a time when swords will be beaten into plowshares and spears into pruning hooks, when nation shall not lift up sword against nation and shall cease to learn war (v. 4). The passage celebrates a vision of peace among countries that have ceased to use their power to control, dominate, oppress, and overpower one another. Hence, they will be liberated from their need to use violence and redeemed from the violence that their actions have created.[6]

Isaiah 32:16–20 describes a vision of peace that can be attained through good leadership. Those who exercise justice and righteousness will cause peace, security, and serenity to flourish. This, in turn, will affect the growth of land to the extent that people will be able to sow beside every stream, and animals will be able to graze freely. Hence, human and nonhuman beings are able to enjoy life when justice and righteousness becomes the lived experience.

Hosea 2:14–23 describes a new covenant that will affect all creation. As mentioned earlier (see chapter 5 above), verses 14–17 speak of a renewed relationship between God and the people, and the people with the land. Verses 18–20, the heart of the passage, describe God's promising to make for the Israelites a covenant "with the wild animals, the birds of the air, and the creeping things of the ground" (v. 18). This covenant recalls the Noachic covenant, which also involved the natural world. Verses 21–23 envision "a day of divine blessing and a time of cosmic salvation."[7] Thus, Hosea 2:14–23 describes a new covenant that will affect all creation positively.[8]

Amos 9:11–15 speaks of restoration and hope (vv. 11–12) and the coming of a new age (vv. 13–15). With metaphorical language, Amos announces the restoration of the kingdom of David and Jerusalem, the place of David's reign (v. 11). Verse 12 suggests that the restored kingdom's borders will extend "to its fullest borders at the time of David...for the nations that were part of the Davidic kingdom at its height were all promised to David and his descendants in God's name (2 Samuel 7)."[9]

---

[6]Cf. Micah 4:1–4.

[7]Dempsey, *The Prophets*, 156.

[8]For a more detailed analysis of Isaiah 2:1–4; 32:16–20; and Hosea 2:14–23, see Dempsey, *The Prophets*, 163, 166, and 155–56, respectively.

[9]Birch, *Hosea, Joel, and Amos*, 256.

Lastly, verses 13–15 contain the promise of a renewed covenant between God and the land, God and the people, and the people and the land.[10]

In summary, Israel's prophets speak of a relationship between humanity's redemption from sin and the restoration of the natural world, as well as the development of harmonious relationships that emerge with a renewed and new sense of covenant. They also speak, however, of a new type of leadership needed to bring to birth the vision of a new creation. In Isaiah 11:1–9, Isaiah envisions this new leader. This person will be connected to the tradition, here specifically to the Davidic line (v. 1), and will be empowered with God's spirit, which will provide the leader with various charismatic gifts needed to fulfill the mission of leadership (v. 2). Love of God will be the leader's delight (v. 3a). Verses 3b–4 describe how the leader will carry out the task of leadership. It will be done with integrity, justice, righteousness, and equity; the leader will exert power through the spoken word, not with weapons or swords, as would be expected in the time of ancient Israel. Verse 5 metaphorically describes the leader's character. Finally, verses 6–9 provide an idyllic picture of what life will be like as a result of the leader's governance. Animals and human beings will live together peacefully on God's holy mountain.

Thus, in 11:1–9, Isaiah envisions a new order whereby the respect and reverence that human beings have for creation is related to the exercise of justice and righteousness among human beings. Isaiah 11:1–9 calls all people, and especially those in leadership positions, to embrace, live out, and govern by a new ethic that insists on responsible living and compassion for all creation—a way of life that flows from one's kinship with all life, and one that acknowledges and celebrates God's faithful love for all that God has created.[11]

Embracing the Prophetic Spirit

The people of ancient Israel lived in hope for a new day, a new time, when there would be a glorious new creation that reflected a life of kinship lived in simple gratitude, reverent awe, and gentle peace. The vision of harmonious and interdependent relationships among all dimensions of creation was and still is the design of the Creator and the dream of the prophets.[12]

In this third millennium, this twenty-first century, Isaiah's prophetic message extends to all people. We are the history-makers, the storytellers,

---

[10]For additional examples that link the redemption of humankind to the restoration of the natural world, see Jeremiah 31:1–6, 10–14; Ezekiel 36:8–12; and Isaiah 33:17–24.

[11]For further discussion on Isaiah 11:1–9, see Dempsey, *The Prophets*, 164–65.

[12]See Genesis 1—2; Isaiah 11:1–9 and 65:17–25; and Hosea 2:16–23.

the poet-prophets of the new day. For the sake of all creation, the vision of Israel's prophets must be kept alive, has to be reread and re-visioned, needs to be heard anew, and cries out to be embraced. Would that this be said about all people:

> Here are my servants, whom I uphold,
> my chosen, in whom my soul delights;
> I have put my spirit upon them;
> they will bring forth justice to the nations.
> They will not cry or lift up their voices,
> or make them heard in the street;
> a bruised reed they will not break,
> and a dimly burning wick they will not quench;
> they will faithfully bring forth justice.
> They will not grow faint or be crushed
> until they have established justice in the earth,
> and the coastlands wait for their teaching.
> (adapted from Isa. 42:1–4)

Empowered by the spirit of the Divine, God's people have the task of bringing forth justice to the nations, which, in the present world setting, suggests action on behalf of underdeveloped nations where justice, righteousness, and equity continue to be the dream of many. The task also suggests action on behalf of those developed nations who need to be reminded that justice, righteousness, and equity are to be privileges for all, not for a few. Finally, when heard amid the sounds of violence and the gasps of pain, the "bruised reed" and the "dimly burning wick" become both the victim of injustice and its perpetrator, who both suffer from oppression and stand in need of justice, compassion, healing, and reconciliation.

Isaiah 42:1–4, then, is a bold reminder that God has entrusted humanity with an ever-ancient, ever-new vision that can no longer remain just a vision. The vision must guide and become the lived reality of humanity if humanity is to be transformed into a "new creation," a community of interdependent relationships.

Isaiah 61:1–4 reinforces the challenges presented in Isaiah 42:1–4. Once addressed to the Judahite community exiled to Babylon in the sixth century B.C.E., and reflective of their experience in exile, 61:1–4 describes the vocation and mission of the prophet, which reaches its full momentum in relation to others' pain and suffering. In the context of contemporary life, the prophet's vocation and mission become a call extended to all people to act on behalf of those oppressed, brokenhearted, captive, and imprisoned, so that once liberated, those who have been suffering can be strengthened and become a living testimony of the power of the Divine Spirit at work in the world, bringing about restoration and transformation. They, in turn, will be gifted with the ongoing mission of restoration and transformation:

> They will be called oaks of righteousness,
> the planting of the LORD, to display his glory.
> They shall build up the ancient ruins,
> they shall raise up the former devastations;
> they shall repair the ruined cities,
> the devastations of many generations. (vv. 3c–4)

Heard in the context of all creation, verses 3c–4 suggest work to be done on behalf of all creation, not just humankind. Looking back on centuries past, the "ancient ruins," "the former devastations," and "the devastations of many generations" include the devastation that humankind has done to the planet—to its ozone layer, its waters, its land, its air, its nonhuman life forms. Verses 3c–4 suggest, then, a vision of restoration for the natural world and for other elements in creation, such as the cities.

Viewed as a whole and heard in a contemporary cosmological setting, Isaiah 61:1–4 suggests to readers that the redemption of humankind is connected to the restoration of the natural world and the transformation of all creation. Additionally, Leviticus 25 is a reminder that "jubilee"—the "year of the Lord's favor" (see Isa. 61:2)— is to be enjoyed by humankind as well as the natural world, that is, the animals and the land. Today, those who mourn are the rivers, the oceans, the streams, the animals, the land, and so forth. All creation needs to be freed from oppression and captivity so that all can enjoy the fullness of life as envisioned by the Creator in the beginning.

In summary, the vision of Israel's prophets offers hope, but it is a hope that is contingent on the willingness of the human community to embrace a way of life and an ethical praxis that affirms creation's intrinsic goodness and assures it of a future shaped by right relationships.

Epilogue

Long ago a child once prayed:
Grandfather,
Look at our brokenness.

We know that in all creation
Only the human family
Has strayed from the Sacred Way.

We know that we are the ones
Who are divided
And we are the ones
Who must come back together
To walk in the Sacred Way.

Grandfather,
Sacred One,
Teach us love, compassion, and honor
That we may heal the earth
And heal each other.[1]

The words of the child's prayer communicate a vision not so different from the one seen and proclaimed by Israel's prophets of old. What the Ojibway Prayer and the prophets have in common is a realization of what was and continues to be—the interconnectedness of life, the suffering of creation, the role that the human family has had in that suffering, and what people must now learn and do to bring about healing and reconciliation, one dimension of the vision of the "new creation."

The message of the prophets, however, is not without its shortcomings, flaws, imperfections, and unsettling images, all of which often betray certain cultural, historical, social, and religious influences that reflect the ancient world and the people's attempt to try to make sense out of their lived

---

[1]"Ojibway Prayer," in *Earth Prayers,* ed. Elizabeth Roberts and Elias Amidon (San Francisco: Harper San Francisco, 1991), 95.

127

experience in relationship to their experience of their God. Yet the prophets' focus on creation, covenant, Torah, and right relationship helps to make the texts' flaws palatable, which allows for the emergence of a timeless and prophetic ethical vision.

Embedded in the ethical message of Israel's prophets is a vision for all creation, one that speaks of the holiness and wholeness of all life with its many interrelated and interdependent relationships. Because the ethical message of Israel's prophets addresses a variety of social injustices present in the ancient world, it strikes a chord with the human community today, which continues to struggle with many of the same social problems that existed centuries ago.

Finally, Israel as a land, a people, and a nation lived to experience what the prophets had warned about—devastation. Some people lived to experience the ash heaps and ruins from the ravages of war and the violence of injustice, and some lived to experience the resettlement in the land and the rebuilding of the temple.

Today the entire planet is God's temple, and all creation is God's community, called to live in right relationship and peace. And although creation suffers and the temple lays in disrepair, today's world is not without hope. The prophet Joel continues to proclaim a word of assurance:

> Do not fear, O soil;
> be glad and rejoice,
> for the LORD has done great things!
> Do not fear, you animals of the field,
> for the pastures of the wilderness are green;
> the tree bears its fruit,
> the fig tree and vine give their full yield. (2:21–22)

Ezekiel also announces a divine promise:

> A new heart I will give you, and a new spirit I will put within you; and I will remove from your body the heart of stone and give you a heart of flesh.(36:26)

This new heart will be

> a heart on fire for the whole of creation, for humanity, for the birds, for the animals, for demons and for all that exists. At the recollection and at the sight of them such a person's eyes overflow with tears owing to vehemence of the compassion which grips his [or her] heart; as a result of his [or her] deep mercy his [or her]

heart shrinks and cannot bear to hear or look on any injury or the slightest suffering of anything in creation.[2]

Would that all humanity experience this new heart. Would that such an experience lead to a cosmic praxis that breaks ground for the new creation that is already unfolding, and whose firstfruits have already been borne in our midst.

---

[2]*Des heiligen Ephraem des Syrers Hymnen de paradiso und contra Julianum*, ed. and trans. Edmund Beck, CSCO 174–75 (Louvain: Secretariat du CorpusSCO, 1957); English translation (with commentary on Genesis, section 2), Sebastian P. Brock, *Hymns on Paradise* (Crestwood, N.Y.: St. Vladimir's Seminary Press, 1990). Also see Dempsey, "Hope Amidst Crisis," 281, where this quote was first used in the context of a discussion on Israel's prophets and ethical praxis.

Select Bibliography

Allen, Leslie. *Ezekiel 1–19.* WordBC, 28. Dallas: Word Books, 1994.

———. *The Books of Joel, Obadiah, Jonah, and Micah.* NICOT. Grand Rapids, Mich.: Eerdmans, 1976.

Andersen, Francis I., and David Noel Freedman. *Amos.* AB 24A. New York: Doubleday, 1989.

———. *Hosea.* AB 24. New York: Doubleday, 1980.

Anderson, Bernhard W. *From Creation to New Creation: Old Testament Perspectives.* OBT. Minneapolis: Fortress Press, 1994.

Bailie, Gil. *Violence Unveiled: Humanity at the Crossroads.* New York: Crossroad, 1997.

Balentine, Samuel E. *The Torah's Vision of Worship.* OBT. Minneapolis: Fortress Press, 1999.

Barstad, Hans M. *The Religious Polemics of Amos.* Leiden, The Netherlands: Brill, 1984.

Barton, John. *Amos's Oracles against the Nations.* New York: Cambridge, 1980.

———. *Ethics and the Old Testament.* London: SCM Press, 1998.

———. "'The Law and the Prophets': Who Are the Prophets?" In *Prophets, Worship, and Theodicy.* Leiden, The Netherlands: Brill, 1984, 1–18.

———. "Prophecy as Ethical Instruction." In *Oracles of God: Perceptions of Ancient Prophecy in Israel after the Exile.* New York: Oxford University, 1986, 154–78.

Bellis, Alice Ogden. *Helpmates, Harlots, and Heroes: Women's Stories in the Hebrew Bible.* Louisville, Ky.: Westminster/John Knox Press, 1994.

Ben Zvi, Ehud. *A Historical-Critical Study of the Book of Obadiah.* New York: de Gruyter, 1996.

Berlin, Adele. *Zephaniah.* AB 25A. New York: Doubleday, 1994.

Berquist, Jon. *Reclaiming Her Story: The Witness of Women in the Old Testament.* St. Louis: Chalice Press, 1992.

Birch, Bruce C. *Hosea, Joel, and Amos.* WestBC. Louisville, Ky.: Westminster John Knox Press, 1997.

———. *Let Justice Roll Down: The Old Testament, Ethics, and Christian Life.* Louisville, Ky.: Westminster/John Knox Press, 1991.

————, Walter Brueggemann, Terence E. Fretheim, and David Petersen. *A Theological Introduction to the Old Testament.* Nashville: Abingdon Press, 1999.

Bird, Phyllis A. *Missing Persons and Mistaken Identities: Women and Gender in Ancient Israel.* OBT. Minneapolis: Fortress Press, 1997.

Blenkinsopp, Joseph. *Ezekiel.* Interpretation. Louisville, Ky.: John Knox Press, 1990.

————. *A History of Prophecy in Israel.* Louisville, Ky.: Westminster John Knox Press, 1996.

————. *Sage, Priest, Prophet: Religious and Intellectual Leadership in Ancient Israel.* Library of Ancient Israel. Louisville, Ky.: Westminster John Knox Press, 1995.

Block, Daniel I. *The Book of Ezekiel: Chapters 1—24.* NICOT. Grand Rapids, Mich.: Eerdmans, 1997.

————. *The Book of Ezekiel: Chapters 25—48.* NICOT. Grand Rapids, Mich.: Eerdmans, 1998.

Bosman, Hendrik. "Adultery, Prophetic Tradition and the Decalogue (1)." In *Wunschet Jerusalem Frieden.* Ed. Matthias Augustin and Klaus-Dietrich Schunck. Beitrage zur Erforschung des Alten Testaments und des Antiken Judentums 13. New York: Lang, 1988, 21–30.

Brache, John M. *Jeremiah 1—29.* WestBC. Louisville, Ky.: Westminster John Knox Press, 2000.

Brenner, Athalya. *A Feminist Companion to the Latter Prophets.* FCB 8. Sheffield, England: Sheffield Academic Press, 1995.

————. *The Israelite Woman: Social Role and Literary Type in Biblical Narrative.* Sheffield, England: JSOT Press, 1985.

Bright, John. *Jeremiah.* AB 21. New York: Doubleday, 1965.

Brown, William. *Obadiah through Malachi.* WestBC. Louisville, Ky.: Westminster John Knox Press, 1996.

Brownlee, William H. *Ezekiel 1—19.* WordBC 28. Waco, Tex.: Word Books, 1986.

Brueggemann, Walter. *A Commentary on Jeremiah: Exile and Homecoming.* Grand Rapids, Mich.: Eerdmans, 1998.

————. *The Covenanted Self: Explorations in Law and Covenant.* Minneapolis: Fortress Press, 1999.

————. *Interpretation and Obedience.* Minneapolis: Fortress Press, 1991.

————. *Isaiah 1—39.* WestBC. Louisville, Ky.: Westminster John Knox Press, 1998.

————. *A Social Reading of the Old Testament: Prophetic Approaches to Israel's Communal Life.* Ed. Patrick D. Miller. Minneapolis: Fortress Press, 1994.

———. *Texts That Linger, Words That Explode: Listening to Prophetic Voices.* Minneapolis: Fortress Press, 2000.

———. *Theology of the Old Testament: Testimony, Dispute, Advocacy.* Minneapolis: Fortress Press, 1997.

———. *To Build and to Plant: Jeremiah 26—52.* ITC. Grand Rapids, Mich.: Eerdmans, 1991.

Bullock, C. Hassell. "The Priestly Era in the Light of Prophetic Thought." In *Israel's Apostasy and Restoration.* Ed. Avraham Gileadi, 1988, 71–78.

Camp, Claudia V., and Carole Fontaine. *Women, War, and Metaphor: Language and Society in the Study of the Hebrew Bible.* Semeia 61. Atlanta: Scholars Press, 1993.

Carley, Keith W. *Ezekiel.* Cambridge, England: Cambridge University Press, 1974.

Carmichael, Calum M. *Law and Narrative in the Bible.* Ithaca, N.Y.: Cornell University, 1985.

Carroll, Robert P. *Jeremiah.* Philadelphia: Westminster Press, 1986.

Carroll Rodas, Mark Daniel. *Contexts for Amos: Prophetic Poetics in Latin American Perspective.* JSOTSup, 132. Sheffield, England: JSOT Press, 1992.

Cheyne, T. K. *Micah.* Cambridge Bible for Schools and Colleges, 27. Cambridge, England: Cambridge University, 1902 (original, 1882).

Clements, Ronald E. *Ezekiel.* WestBC. Louisville, Ky.: Westminster John Knox Press, 1996.

——— . *Isaiah 1—39.* NCBC (Grand Rapids, Mich.: Eerdmans, 1980).

———. *Jeremiah.* Interpretation. Louisville, Ky.: Westminster/ John Knox Press, 1988.

Clifford, Richard J. "The Use of Hôy in the Prophets" *CBQ* 28 (1966): 458–64.

———. *Jeremiah.* Interpretation. Atlanta: John Knox Press, 1988.

Clines, David J. A. *Interested Parties: The Ideology of Writers and Readers of the Hebrew Bible.* JSOTSup 205; Gender, Culture, Theory 1. Sheffield, England: Sheffield Academic Press, 1995.

Cody, Aelred. *Ezekiel with an Excursus on Old Testament Priesthood.* OTM 11. Wilmington, Del.: Glazier, 1984.

Conrad, Edgar W. *Reading Isaiah.* OBT. Minneapolis: Fortress Press, 1991.

Cooke, G. A. *The Book of Ezekiel.* ICC. Edinburgh, Scotland: T. & T. Clark, 1985.

Cooper, Lamar Eugene. *Ezekiel.* NAC 17. Nashville: Broadman & Holman, 1994.

Crenshaw, James L., and John T. Willis, eds. *Essays in Old Testament Ethics.* New York: KTAV, 1974.

————. *Joel.* AB 24C. New York: Doubleday, 1964.

Crüsemann, Frank. *The Torah: Theology and Social History of the Old Testament Law.* Trans. Allan W. Mahnke. Minneapolis: Fortress Press, 1996, 2.

Darr, Katheryn Pfisterer. *Isaiah's Vision and the Family of God.* Louisville, Ky.: Westminster John Knox Press, 1994.

Davies, Eryl W. *Prophecy and Ethics: Isaiah and the Ethical Tradition of Israel.* JSOTSup 16. Sheffield, England: JSOT Press, 1981.

Davies, G. I. *Hosea.* NCBC. Grand Rapids, Mich.: Eerdmans, 1992.

Davies, Philip R. *The Prophets: A Sheffield Reader.* The Biblical Seminar 42. Sheffield, England: Sheffield Academic Press, 1996.

————, and David J. A. Clines, eds. *Among the Prophets: Language, Image, and Structure in the Prophetic Writings.* JSOTSup 144. Sheffield, England: JSOT Press, 1993.

Day, Peggy L., ed. *Gender and Difference in Ancient Israel.* Minneapolis: Fortress Press, 1989.

Dearman, John Andrew. "The Blessing of Torah: Preaching the Gospel Beforehand." *Austin Seminary Bulletin: Faculty Edition* (1990): 33–50.

————. *Property Rights in the Eighth-Century Prophets: The Conflict and Its Background.* SBLDS 106. Atlanta: Scholars Press, 1988.

————. *Religion and Culture in Ancient Israel.* Peabody, Mass.: Hendrickson, 1992.

Dempsey, Carol J. "Hope Amidst Crisis: A Prophetic Vision of Cosmic Redemption." In *All Creation Is Groaning: An Interdisciplinary Vision for Life in a Sacred Universe.* Ed. Carol J. Dempsey and Russell A. Butkus. Collegeville, Minn.: Liturgical Press, 1999, 269–84.

————. "The Interplay between Literary Form and Technique and Ethics in Micah 1—3." Ph.D. diss., The Catholic University of America, 1994.

————. "Micah 2—3: Literary Artistry, Ethical Message, and Some Considerations about the Image of YHWH and Micah," *JSOT* 85 (1999): 21–30.

————. *The Prophets: A Liberation-Critical Reading.* Minneapolis: Fortress Press, 2000.

————. "The 'Whore' of Ezekiel 16: The Impact and Ramifications of Gender-Specific Metaphors in Light of Biblical Law and Divine Judgment." In *Gender and Law in the Hebrew Bible and the Ancient Near East.* Ed. Victor Matthews, Bernard M. Levinson, and Tikva Frymer-Kensky. JSOTSup 262. Sheffield, England: Sheffield Academic Press, 1998, 55–76.

————, and Russell A. Butkus, eds. *All Creation Is Groaning: An Interdisciplinary Vision for Life in a Sacred Universe*. Collegeville, Minn.: Liturgical Press, 1999.

Doorly, William J. *Prophet of Justice: Understanding the Book of Amos*. Mahwah, N.J.: Paulist Press, 1989.

Dowd, Michael. *Earthspirit: A Handbook for Nurturing an Ecological Christianity*. Mystic, Conn.: Twenty-Third Publications, 1991.

Eichrodt, Walther. *Ezekiel*. OTL. Philadelphia: Westminster Press, 1970.

Eideval, Goran. *Grapes in the Desert: Metaphors, Models, and Themes in Hosea 4—14*. Stockholm, Sweden: Almqvist & Wiksell International, 1996.

Emmerson, Grace I. *Isaiah 56—66*. OTG. Sheffield, England: JSOT Press, 1992.

————. "Women in Ancient Israel." In *The World of Ancient Israel: Sociological, Anthropological and Political Perspectives*. Ed. R. E. Clements. New York: Cambridge University, 1989, 371–94.

Ephrem of Syria, Saint. *Des heiligen Ephraem des Syrers Hymnen de paradiso und contra Julianum*. Ed. and trans. Edmund Beck. CSCO 174–75. Louvain: Secretariat du CorpusSCO, 1957. English: *Hymns on Paradise*. Trans. Sebastian P. Brock. Crestwood, N.Y.: St. Vladimir's Seminary Press, 1990.

Follis, Elaine R., ed. "The Holy City as Daughter." In *Directions in Biblical Hebrew Poetry*. JSOTSup 40. Sheffield, England: JSOT Press, 1987, 173–84.

Franke, Chris. *Isaiah 46, 47, and 48: A New Literary-Critical Reading*. Biblical and Judaic Studies 3. Winona Lake, Ind.: Eisenbrauns, 1994.

Fretheim, Terence E. *The Suffering of God: An Old Testament Perspective*. OBT. Philadelphia: Fortress Press, 1984.

Gaffney Edward McGlynn, Jr. "Of Covenants Ancient and New: The Influence of Secular Law on Biblical Religion." *JLR* 2 (1984): 117–44.

Gerstenberger, Erhard S. *Yahweh the Patriarch: Ancient Images of God and Feminist Theology*. Trans. Frederick J. Gaiser. Minneapolis: Fortress Press, 1996.

Girard, Rene. *Violence and the Sacred*. Trans. P. Gregory. Baltimore: Johns Hopkins University, 1977.

Gitay, Yehoshua. *Isaiah and His Audience: The Structure and Meaning of Isaiah 1—12*. Studia Semitica Neerlandica. The Netherlands: Van Gorcum, 1991.

Gordon, Robert P., ed. *The Place Is Too Small for Us: The Israelite Prophets in Recent Scholarship*. Sources for Biblical and Theological Study 5. Winona Lake, Ind.: Eisenbrauns, 1995.

Gossai, Hemchand. *Justice, Righteousness and the Social Critique of the Eighth-Century Prophets*. American University Studies: Series 7. Theology and Religion, vol. 141. New York: Peter Lang, 1993.

Gottwald, Norman K., ed. *The Bible and Liberation*. Maryknoll, N.Y.: Orbis Books, 1989.

————. *The Hebrew Bible in Its Social World and in Ours*. The Society of Biblical Literaure, Semeia Studies. Atlanta: Scholars Press, 1993.

————. *The Tribes of Yahweh: A Sociology of the Religion of Liberated Israel, 1250—1050 B.C.E.* Maryknoll, N.Y.: Orbis Books, 1979.

Gowan, Donald. *Theology of the Prophetic Books: The Death and Resurrection of Israel*. Louisville, Ky.: Westminster John Knox Press, 1998.

Granberg-Michaelson, Wesley. "Covenant and Creation." In *Liberating Life: Contemporary Approaches to Ecological Thinking*. Ed. Charles Birch, William Eakin, and Jay B. McDaniel. Maryknoll, N.Y.: Orbis Books, 1990, 2–36.

Gray, G. B. *A Critical and Exegetical Commentary on the Book of Isaiah I—XXVII* . ICC. Edinburgh, Scotland: T. & T. Clark, 1912.

Greenberg, Moshe. *Ezekiel 1—20*. AB 22. Garden City, N.Y.: Doubleday, 1983.

Griffin, William Paul. *The God of the Prophets: An Analysis of Divine Action*. JSOTSup 249. Sheffield, England: Sheffield Academic Press, 1997.

Halkes, Catharina J. M. *New Creation: Christian Feminism and the Renewal of the Earth*. Trans. Catherine Romanik. Louisville, Ky.: Westminster/John Knox Press, 1991.

Hall, Douglas John, and Rosemary Radford Ruether. *God and the Nations*. Minneapolis: Fortress Press, 1995.

Halpern, Baruch, and Deborah W. Hobson, eds. *Law and Ideology in Monarchic Israel*. JSOTSup 124. Sheffield, England: JSOT Press, 1991.

Hals, R. M. *Ezekiel*. FOTL 12. Grand Rapids, Mich.: Eerdmans, 1989.

Hanson, Paul D. *Isaiah 40—66*. Interpretation. Louisville, Ky.: Westminster John Knox Press, 1995.

Harper, William Rainey. *A Critical and Exegetical Commentary on Amos and Hosea*. ICC. Edinburgh, Scotland: T. & T. Clark, repr. 1979.

Hillers, Delbert R. *Lamentations*. AB, 7A. Garden City, N.Y.: Doubleday, 1972.

————. *Micah*. Hermeneia. Philadelphia: Fortress Press, 1984.

Holladay, William L. *Isaiah: Scroll of a Prophetic Heritage*. Grand Rapids, Mich.: Eerdmans, 1978.

————. *Jeremiah 1*. Hermeneia. Philadelphia: Fortress Press, 1986.

————. *Jeremiah 2*. Hermeneia. Minneapolis: Fortress Press, 1989.

————. *Long Ago God Spoke: How Christians May Hear the Old Testament Today*. Minneapolis: Fortress Press, 1995.

Huey, F. B., Jr. *Jeremiah—Lamentations*. NAC 16. Nashville: Broadman & Holman, 1993.

Huffmon, Herbert B. "The Social Role of Amos' Message." In *The Quest for the Kingdom of God: Studies in Honor of George E. Mendenhall*. Ed. H. B. Huffmon, F. A. Spina, and A. R. W. Green. Winona Lake, Ind.: Eisenbrauns, 1983, 109–16.

Janzen, Waldemar. *Old Testament Ethics: A Paradigmatic Approach*. Louisville, Ky.: Westminster/John Knox Press, 1994.

Jensen, Joseph. *Isaiah 1—39*. OTM 8. Wilmington, Del.: Glazier, 1984.

Johnson, Elizabeth. *Women, Earth, and Creator Spirit*. Mahwah, N.J.: Paulist Press, 1993.

Jones, Douglas Rawlinson. *Jeremiah*. NCBC. Grand Rapids, Mich.: Eerdmans, 1992.

Kaiser, Otto. *Introduction to the Old Testament*. Trans. J. Sturdy. Minneapolis: Augsburg Press, 1975.

———. *Isaiah 1—12*. Trans. John Bowden. OTL. Philadelphia: Westminster Press, 1983.

———. *Isaiah 13—39: A Commentary*. Trans. R. A. Wilson. OTL. Philadelphia: Westminster Press, 1974.

Kaiser, Walter C. *Toward Old Testament Ethics*. Grand Rapids, Mich.: Zondervan, 1983.

Kaminski, Joel S. *Corporate Responsibility in the Hebrew Bible*. JSOTSup 196. Sheffield, England: Sheffield Academic Press, 1995.

Kapelrud, Arvid S. "The Prophets and the Covenant." In *The Shelter of Elyon: Essays on Ancient Palestinian Life and Literature*. Ed. W. Boyd Barrick and John R. Spencer. JSOTSup 31. Sheffield, England: JSOT Press, 1984, 175–83.

Klein, Ralph W. *Israel in Exile: A Theological Interpretation*. OBT. Philadelphia: Fortress Press, 1979.

Laffey, Alice L. *An Introduction to the Old Testament: A Feminist Perspective*. Philadelphia: Fortress Press, 1988.

———. *The Pentateuch: A Liberation Critical Reading*. Minneapolis: Fortress Press, 1998.

Landy, Francis. *Hosea*. Sheffield, England: Sheffield Academic Press, 1995.

Lang, B. "Peasant Poverty in Biblical Israel," *JSOT* 24 (1982): 54.

Larsson, Goran. *Bound for Freedom: The Book of Exodus in Jewish and Christian Traditions*. Peabody, Mass.: Hendrickson, 1999.

Limburg, James. *Hosea—Micah*. Interpretation. Atlanta: John Knox Press, 1988.

———. *Jonah*. Louisville, Ky.: Westminster/John Knox Press, 1993.

Lundbom, Jack R. *Jeremiah: A Study in Ancient Hebrew Rhetoric*. Winona Lake, Ind.: Eisenbrauns, 1997.

Lundquist, John M. "Temple, Covenant, and Law in the Ancient Near East and in the Old Testament." In *Israel's Apostasy and Restoration*. Grand Rapids, Mich.: Baker, 1988, 293–305.

McConville, J. G. *Judgment and Promise: An Interpretation of the Book of Jeremiah.* Winona Lake, Ind.: Eisenbrauns, 1993.

————. *Law and Theology in Deuteronomy.* JSOTSup 33. Sheffield, England: JSOT Press, 1984.

McCoy, Charles S. "Creation and Covenant: A Comprehensive Vision for Environmental Ethics." In *Covenant for a New Creation: Ethics, Religion, and Public Policy*. Ed. Carol S. Robb and Carl J. Casebolt. Maryknoll, N.Y.: Orbis Books, 1991, 212–25.

McKeating, Henry. *The Books of Amos, Hosea and Micah.* CBC. Cambridge, England: Cambridge University Press, 1971.

McKenzie, John L. *Second Isaiah.* AB 20. New York: Doubleday, 1968.

Malchow, Bruce V. *Social Justice in the Hebrew Bible.* Collegeville, Minn.: Michael Glazier/Liturgical Press, 1996.

Mamul Malul. "Adoption of Foundlings in the Bible and Mesopotamian Documents: A Study of Some Legal Metaphors in Ezekiel 16.1–7." *JSOT* 46 (1990): 97–126.

Matthews, Victor H., and Don C. Benjamin, *Social World of Ancient Israel 1250–587 BCE*. Peabody, Mass.: Hendrickson, 1993.

Mayes, Andrew. "Prophecy and Society in Israel." In *Of Prophets' Visions and the Wisdom of Sages*. JSOTSup 162. Ed. Heather A. McKay and David J. A. Clines. Sheffield, England: JSOT Press, 1993, 25–42.

Mays, James Luther. *Amos.* OTL. Philadelphia: Westminster Press, 1969.

————. *Micah.* OTL. Philadelphia: Westminster Press, 1976.

Meyers, Carol L., and Eric M. Meyers. *Haggai, Zechariah 1–8.* AB 25B. Garden City, N.Y.: Doubleday, 1987.

————. *Zechariah 9—14.* AB 25C. New York: Doubleday, 1964.

Milgrom, Jacob. *Leviticus 1—16.* AB 3. New York: Doubleday, 1991.

Millar, J. Gary. *Now Choose Life: Theology and Ethics in Deuteronomy*. New Studies in Biblical Theology. Grand Rapids, Mich.: Eerdmans, 1998.

Mills, Mary E. *Images of God in the Old Testament*. Collegeville, Minn.: Liturgical Press, 1998.

Miscall, Peter D. *Isaiah.* Sheffield, England: JSOT Press, 1993.

Moore, Carey A. *Daniel, Esther and Jeremiah: The Additions*. Garden City, N.Y.: Doubleday, 1977.

Morris, Gerald. *Prophecy, Poetry and Hosea.* JSOTSup 219. Sheffield, England: Sheffield Academic Press, 1996.

Mott, Stephen Charles. "God's Justice and Ours." In *Biblical Ethics and Social Change*. New York: Oxford University Press, 1982, 59–81.

Motyer, J. Alec. *The Prophecy of Isaiah: An Introduction and Commentary.* Downers Grove, Ill.: InterVarsity Press, 1993.

Murray, Robert. *The Cosmic Covenant: Biblical Themes of Justice and Peace, and the Integrity of Creation.* Heythrop Monographs. London, England: Sheed & Ward, 1992.

————. "Prophecy and the Cult." In *Israel's Prophetic Tradition.* Ed. Richard Coggins, Anthony Phillips, and Michael Knibb. New York: Cambridge University Press, 1982, 200–216.

Neiderhiser, E. A., "Micah 2:6–11: Considerations on the Nature of the Discourse," *BTB* 11 (1981): 104–7.

Newsom, Carol A., and Sharon H. Ringe, eds. *The Women's Bible Commentary.* Expanded ed. with Apocrypha. Louisville, Ky.: Westminster John Knox Press, 1998.

Niditch, Susan. *Ancient Israelite Religion.* New York: Oxford University Press, 1997.

————. *War in the Hebrew Bible: A Study in the Ethics of Violence.* New York: Oxford University Press, 1993.

Nielsen, Kirsten. *There Is Hope for a Tree: The Tree as Metaphor in Isaiah.* Trans. Christine and Frederick Crowley. JSOTSup 65. Sheffield, England: JSOT Press, 1989.

North, C. R. *The Second Isaiah: Introduction, Translation, and Commentary to Chapters XL—LV.* Oxford: Clarendon, 1964.

Nowell, Irene. "Jonah." In *Collegeville Bible Commentary.* Ed. Dianne Bergant. Collegeville, Minn.: Liturgical Press, 1992, 828–31.

"Ojibway Prayer." In *Earth Prayers.* Ed. Elizabeth Roberts and Elias Amidon. San Francisco: Harper San Francisco, 1991, 95.

Olyan, Saul M., "The Oaths of Amos 8:14." In *Priesthood and Cult in Ancient Israel.* Ed. Gary A. Anderson and Saul M. Olyan. JSOTSup 125. Sheffield, England: Sheffield Academic Press, 1991, 121–49.

Ortlund, Raymond C., Jr. *Whoredom: God's Unfaithful Wife in Biblical Theology.* NSBT. Grand Rapids, Mich.: Eerdmans, 1996.

Oswalt, John N. *The Book of Isaiah: Chapters 1—39.* NICOT. Grand Rapids, Mich.: Eerdmans, 1986.

————. *The Book of Isaiah: Chapters 40—66.* NICOT. Grand Rapids, Mich.: Eerdmans, 1998.

Paul, Shalom M. *Amos.* Hermeneia. Minneapolis: Fortress Press, 1991.

Petersen, David L. *Haggai and Zechariah 1—8.* OTL. Philadelphia: Westminster Press, 1984.

————. *Zechariah 9—14 and Malachi.* OTL. Louisville, Ky.: Westminster John Knox Press, 1995.

Phillips, Anthony. "Prophecy and Law." In *Israel's Prophetic Tradition*. Ed. Richard Coggins, Anthony Phillips, and Michael Knibb. New York: Cambridge University Press, 1982, 217–32.

Preuss, Horst Dietrich. *Old Testament Theology*. Vol. 1. OTL. Louisville, Ky.: Westminster John Knox Press, 1995.

———. *Old Testament Theology*. Vol. 2. OTL. Louisville, Ky.: Westminster John Knox Press, 1996.

Prinsloo, Willem S. *The Theology of the Book of Joel*. New York: de Gruyter, 1985.

Raabe, Paul R. *Obadiah*. AB 24D. New York: Doubleday, 1996.

Reid, Stephen Breck, ed. *Prophets and Paradigms*. JSOTSup 229. Sheffield, England: Sheffield Academic Press, 1996.

Reviv, Hanoch. "The Priesthood as a Political Pressure-Group in Judah." In *Wunschet Jerusalem Frieden*. Ed. Matthias Augustin and Klaus-Dietrich Schunck. Beitrage Zur Erforschung Des Alten Testaments Und Des Antiken Judentums 13. New York: Lang, 1988, 205–10.

Ringgren, Helmer. "Prophecy in the Ancient Near East." In *Israel's Prophetic Tradition*. Ed. Richard Coggins, Anthony Phillips, and Michael Knibb. New York: Cambridge University Press, 1982, 1–11.

Robb, Carol S., and Carl J. Casebolt. "Introduction." In *Covenant for a New Creation: Ethics, Religion, and Public Policy*. Ed. Carol S. Robb and Carl J. Casebolt. Maryknoll, N.Y.: Orbis Books, 1991, 1–23.

Roberts, J. J. M. *Nahum, Habakkuk, and Zephaniah*. OTL. Louisville, Ky.: Westminster/John Knox Press, 1991.

Robertson, O. Palmer. *The Books of Nahum, Habakkuk, and Zephaniah*. NICOT. Grand Rapids, Mich.: Eerdmans, 1990.

Russell, David M. *The "New Heavens and New Earth": Hope for the Creation in Jewish Apocalyptic and the New Testament*. Studies in Biblical Apocalyptic Literature 1. Philadelphia: Visionary Press, 1996.

Sakenfeld, Katharine Doob. *Faithfulness in Action: Loyalty in Biblical Perspective*. OBT. Philadelphia: Fortress Press, 1985.

Sanders, James A. *Torah and Canon*. Philadelphia: Fortress Press, 1972, 2.

Schmitt, John J. "The Gender of Ancient Israel," *JSOT* 26 (1983): 115–25.

Schubeck, Thomas L. *Liberation Ethics*. Minneapolis: Fortress Press, 1993.

Schwager, Raymund. *Must There Be Scapegoats? Violence and Redemption in the Bible*. Trans. Maria J. Assad. San Francisco: Harper & Row, 1987.

Schwartz, Howard Eilberg. *The Savage in Judaism: An Anthropology of Israelite Religion and Ancient Judaism*. Indianapolis: Indiana University Press, 1990.

Scott, R. B. Y. "The Theology of the Prophets." In *The Relevance of the Prophets*. New York: Macmillan, 1968, 114–41.

————."The Prophets and History." In *The Relevance of the Prophets*. New York: Macmillan 1968, 142–70.

————. "The Prophets and the Social Order." In *The Relevance of the Prophets*. New York: Macmillan 1968, 171–92.

Segovia, Fernando F., and Mary Ann Tolbert, eds. *Reading from This Place*. Vol. 1. *Social Location and Biblical Interpretation in the United States*. Minneapolis: Fortress Press, 1995.

————. *Reading from This Place*. Vol. 2. *Social Location and Biblical Interpretation in Global Perspective*. Minneapolis: Fortress Press, 1995.

Seitz, Christopher R. *Isaiah 1—39*. Interpretation. Louisville, Ky.: Westminster/John Knox Press, 1993.

Sherwin, Byron L. "Law and Love in Jewish Theology." *ATR* 64 (19):468.

Simkins, Ronald A. *Creator and Creation*. Peabody, Mass.: Hendrickson, 1994.

————. *Yahweh's Activity in History and Nature in the Book of Joel*. ANET 10. Lewiston, N.Y.: Edwin Mellen Press, 1991.

Smith, John Merlin Powis, et al. *Micah, Zephaniah, Nahum, Habakkuk, Obadiah and Joel*. ICC 24. Edinburgh, Scotland: T. & T. Clark, 1911 [reprinted 1985].

Smith, Mark S. *The Early History of God: Yahweh and the Other Deities in Ancient Israel*. San Francisco: Harper & Row, 1987.

Smith, Ralph L. *Micah-Malachi*. WordBC 32. Waco, Tex.: Word Books, 1984.

————. *Old Testament Theology: Its History, Method, and Message*. Nashville: Broadman & Holman, 1993.

Sobosan, Jeffrey G. *Bless the Beasts: A Spirituality for Animal Care*. New York: Crossroad, 1991.

Stuart, Douglas. *Hosea-Jonah*. WordBC 31. Waco, Tex.: Word Books, 1987.

Sweeney, Marvin A. *Isaiah 1—39 with an Introduction to Prophetic Literature*. FOTL 16. Grand Rapids, Mich.: Eerdmans, 1996.

Talmon, S. *Storia e Tradizioni di Israele*. Ed. D. Garrone and F. Israel. Brescia: Paideia Editrice, 1991.

Trible, Phyllis. *God and the Rhetoric of Sexuality*. OBT. Philadelphia: Fortress Press, 1978.

Ulrich, Eugene, John W. Wright, Robert P. Carroll, and Philip R. Davies, eds. *Priests, Prophets and Scribes: Essays on the Formation and Heritage of Second Temple Judaism in Honour of Joseph Blenkinsopp*. JSOTSup 149. Sheffield, England: JSOT Press, 1992.

Verhoef, Pieter A. *The Books of Haggai and Malachi*. Grand Rapids, Mich.: Eerdmans, 1987.

Waldo, H. Eberhard von. "Social Responsibility and Social Structure in Early Israel," *CBQ* 32 (1970): 182–204.

Walsh, J. P. M. *The Mighty from Their Thrones: Power in the Biblical Tradition.* OBT. Philadelphia: Fortress Press, 1987.

Waltke, Bruce K., et al. *Obadiah, Jonah, and Micah.* The Tyndale Old Testament Commentaries. Downers Grove, Ill.: InterVarsity Press, 1988.

Watson, Francis. *Text, Church, and World.* Grand Rapids, Mich.: Eerdmans, 1994.

Watts, John D. W. "Babylonian Idolatry in the Prophets as a False Socio-Economic System." In *Israel's Apostasy and Restoration.* Ed. Avraham Gileadi. Grand Rapids, Mich.: Baker, 1988, 115–22.

———. *Isaiah 1—33.* WordBC 24. Waco, Tex.: Word Books, 1985.

———. *Isaiah 34—66.* WordBC 25. Waco, Tex.: Word Books, 1987.

Weems, Renita J. *Battered Love: Marriage, Sex, and Violence in the Hebrew Prophets.* Minneapolis: Fortress Press, 1995.

Weinfeld, Moshe. *Deuteronomy and the Deuteronomic School.* Winona Lake, Ind.: Eisenbrauns, 1992.

———. *Social Justice in Ancient Israel and in the Ancient Near East.* Minneapolis: Fortress Press, 1995.

Weiss, Meir. "The Decalogue in Prophetic Literature." In *The Ten Commandments in History and Tradition.* Ed. Gershon Levi. Jerusalem: Magnes, 1990.

Wessels, W. J. "Conflicting Powers: Reflections from the Book of Micah," *Old Testament Essays* 10, no. 3 (1997): 539.

Westermann, Claus. *Isaiah 40—66.* OTL. Trans. David M. Stalker. Philadelphia: Westminster Press, 1969.

———. *Lamentations: Issues and Interpretation.* Trans. Charles Muenchow. Minneapolis: Fortress Press, 1994.

Wevers, John W. *Ezekiel.* NCBC. Grand Rapids, Mich.: Eerdmans, 1969.

Wilson, Robert R. *Prophecy and Society in Ancient Israel.* Philadelphia: Fortress Press, 1980.

Witaszek, G. *Provocy Amos i Micheasz wobec niesprawiedl i wosci spolecznej.* Tuchow: Mala Poligrafia oo. Redemtorystow, 1992.

Wolff, Hans Walter. *Haggai.* Trans. Margaret Kohl. Minneapolis: Augsburg Press, 1988.

———. *Hosea.* Hermeneia. Trans. Gary Stansell. Philadelphia: Fortress Press, 1974.

———. *Joel and Amos.* Hermeneia. Trans. Waldemar Janzen, S. Dean McBride, Jr., and Charles A. Muenchow. Philadelphia: Fortress Press, 1977.

———. *Micah.* Trans. Gary Stansell. Minneapolis: Augsburg Press, 1990.

————. *Obadiah and Jonah*. Trans. Margaret Kohl. Minneapolis: Augsburg Press, 1986.

————. "What Is New in the New Covenant." *Confrontations with Prophets*. Philadelphia: Fortress Press, 1983, 49–62.

Woods, John A. *Perspectives on War in the Bible*. Macon, Ga.: Mercer University Press, 1998.

Woude, A. S. van der. "Micah in Dispute with the Pseudo-Prophets," *VT* 19 (1960): 244–60.

Yee, Gale A. "Hosea." In *Women's Bible Commentary*. Expanded ed. with Apocrypha. Ed. Carol A. Newsom and Sharon H. Ringe. Louisville, Ky.: Westminster John Knox Press, 1998, 207–15.

Zimmerli, Walther. *Ezekiel 1*. Hermeneia. Trans. Ronald E. Clements. Philadelphia: Fortress Press, 1979.

————. *Ezekiel 2*. Hermeneia. Trans. James D. Martin. Philadelphia: Fortress Press, 1983.

Scripture Index

Author Index

Subject Index